CW01337496

THE HISTORY OF WESTMINSTER SYNAGOGUE

1. *Kent House, from an oil painting, 1961, by Bill Benson, a founder member of the congregation*

THE HISTORY OF WESTMINSTER SYNAGOGUE

PHILIPPA BERNARD

To Azia + Suzy
with all good wishes
Philippa

WESTMINSTER SYNAGOGUE

2003

Published by
Westminster Synagogue
Kent House
Rutland Gardens
Knightsbridge
London
SW7 1BX

ISBN 0-9518708-4-X

Designed and typeset by
Libanus Press Ltd
Marlborough, Wiltshire

Printed by
B·A·S Printers Ltd
Salisbury, Wiltshire

This book is dedicated to
founder members of Westminster Synagogue

CONTENTS

FOREWORD

Westminster Synagogue is a relatively young congregation but since its formation it has nonetheless made a significant contribution to Anglo-Jewry.

The synagogue has now reached the stage where many members, not just those who have recently joined, are not fully aware of its background, and we are extremely grateful to Philippa Bernard for writing its history. Included in this book is an informative account of Kent House itself, and as the building has been recently refurbished, we can look forward to a growing congregation, active both within our own membership and as part of the wider community.

HOWARD LEIGH
January, 2003

INTRODUCTION

When Westminster Synagogue came into being (as the New London Jewish Congregation) in 1957, many of those who were responsible for its establishment, were young, lively and deeply committed to its principles and policy. Inevitably, memories of those early days are fading, and younger members may know little about the origins of the congregation and its acquisition of Kent House. It is for this reason that the present work has been undertaken. It seemed to me to be important, before it is too late, to try to capture the feelings of excitement and commitment experienced by those who formed the congregation, as well as the continued loyalty and hard work of those who carried it on.

Three rabbis in some forty-six years is not a bad record; each has led the congregation in his own fashion, each has been loved and respected. Each rabbi's wife, too, has played her individual part in the synagogue's progress, preserving, as it happens, a tradition at Kent House, where earlier chatelaines – women of character and nobility – each governed the house in her own inimitable way.

This book, which simply set out to tell the story of the congregation, took on a life of its own when the earlier history of the building, so great an influence in that story, began to expand voluminously. I have therefore relegated that early history to a separate section after the main story has been told.

Many members have lively personal recollections of synagogue life and a few of these have been included in the book.

It has not been possible in this narrative to mention all those who played a significant part in the congregation's story, but it need hardly be said that every one of those who have given the synagogue a place in their lives can take pride in its progress – and in its possession of a beautiful and historic house.

I have often referred to generous gifts made to the synagogue, but in accordance with our long-standing policy, I have named only those donors who were not members of the congregation.

Many who read the book will, I feel sure, point out omissions and mistakes. For these I apologise – I alone am responsible for them. I have tried to avoid contention and acrimony, while including differences of opinion where they occurred.

I have received help from more people than I can possibly name: from the West London Synagogue and the London Metropolitan Archives; from Rabbi Friedlander and Rabbi Salamon; from many members, young and old; from Lewis and Jacqueline Golden, who read the manuscript; and most of all from my husband Leo who was 'in at the beginning' and kept me in check.

PHILIPPA BERNARD

LIST OF ILLUSTRATIONS

CHAPTER I

IN THE BEGINNING

On 15 April 1840, a meeting was held at the Bedford Hotel, at which were present twenty-four London Jews, eighteen from the Sephardi and six from the Ashkenazi communities. The only Sephardi synagogue in London at that time was Bevis Marks in the City, and as the congregants prospered and moved to homes and businesses further to the west, it became inevitably less convenient for them to attend services. The ruling body of Sephardi Jews, the Mahamad, was accordingly requested to authorise the foundation of another synagogue further to the west as a more accessible place of worship. This it steadfastly refused to do.

The influential Anglo-Jewish families who had come together to discuss the possibility of secession (nine of the twenty-four were Mocattas, three were Montefiores and three Henriques), were dissatisfied in other ways. Decorum at services left much to be desired, the services were inordinately long, with sermons in Hebrew, and there was virtually no religious instruction for children. The Ashkenazim present were of similar mind, and after considerable debate the meeting resolved that in spite of the wishes of the parent synagogue at Bevis Marks, those present would found a new congregation in a convenient part of London, to be called The Synagogue of British Jews ('West London' was added later). The name was chosen to avoid any conflict between Sephardim and Ashkenazim and to stress the common aspirations of the two communities. Services were to conform to those familiar to the majority of congregants, with the liturgy mainly in Hebrew, according to the Sephardi pronunciation, but with sermons in English. Sabbath services would commence at 9.30 am in the summer and

10 am in winter, lasting no more than two-and-a-half hours, and congregants would be expected to arrive at the beginning and stay to the end. Thus did the first Reform synagogue in Great Britain come into being.

Considerable attention was given to the conduct of the minister and to that of the worshippers, who were to act 'in a manner which may appear best calculated to excite feelings of devotion'. The position of minister was offered to a distinguished scholar from the Liverpool Ashkenazi Synagogue, the Rev. David Woolf Marks. It is interesting to note that Rev. Marks' granddaughter, Mary Ann Southam (née Marks) was a founder member of Westminster Synagogue.

It took two years for the newly established congregation to find its feet. The Board of Deputies of British Jews refused to give Rev. Marks permission to conduct marriages and a particularly aggravating problem was the hostility of Bevis Marks, even though the Mahamad had tried to prevent a split in the ranks by offering to open another synagogue under its own auspices. When this offer was refused the Ashkenazi Chief Rabbi and the head of the Sephardi community (the Haham) issued a 'cherem' excommunicating the renegades; it was not lifted for seven years.

The first home of the new congregation was in Burton Street, near Tavistock Square. Under the guidance of the minister a new prayer book was compiled but some of the more radical ideas took some time to become accepted. It was not until 1859, when the synagogue moved to Margaret Street, that an organ was installed, and even after the move to a splendid new building in Upper Berkeley Street in 1870, men and women still sat separately. This did not change for Sabbath services until after the First World War, and is still maintained for practical reasons on the High Holydays.

In the early years of the twentieth century a certain lack of involvement and spontaneity made itself felt in the conduct of the synagogue. It was still governed by the old Anglo-Jewish families, but they did not expect their membership to play too demanding a part in their lives. Morris Joseph, whose distinguished ministry had served the synagogue so well, was in his eighties, and in 1929 Philip Waley, whose family had long been associated with the Reform movement, was dispatched to America to seek a new rabbi for the rapidly-growing congregation. The man he brought back to the West London Synagogue was a graduate of the Hebrew Union College, Harold Frederic Reinhart, with his 'sweet little Russian wife Flora'. He had served congregations in Gary, Baton Rouge and Sacramento, and set about his ministry in London with the vigour and devotion that was characteristic of everything he did.

It took only five years for Rabbi Reinhart's enthusiasm to transform the congregation. His interest in education and youth activities, and his skill in administration, inspired the construction of an annexe in Seymour Place, incorporating the Stern Hall, new offices, classrooms and a room of prayer. This small sanctuary meant much to him, and he held a short service there every evening at 6.30 which everyone in the building at the time was encouraged to attend. The fifteen-minute services were simple but moving, consisting only of one or two psalms, the Shema and Amidah, and a closing Kaddish. The opening of this new annexe was attended by the Chief Rabbi, Joseph Hertz, whose affection and regard for Harold Reinhart was followed by that of Israel Brodie in later years.

Other matters which exercised the senior minister in the early years were the regular appearance of *The Synagogue Review*, which he edited, a greatly expanded religion school, a Junior Membership for the 16 to 25 age group, and a lively programme of events including music, lectures and social activities of every kind.

Under Harold Reinhart's leadership, the influence of Berkeley Street on like-minded Jews all over Britain was making itself felt. Reform congregations had been founded in Manchester and Bradford during the nineteenth century. The first London Reform synagogue to be founded after West London was at Golders Green in 1933. Rabbi Reinhart greeted its early needs with his invariable enthusiasm, arranging financial help, providing Sifre Torah, and writing to families in the neighbourhood to commend the new project. A parcel of land at Hoop Lane owned by the West London Synagogue was made available and the North Western Reform Synagogue came into being at Alyth Gardens. In the same year Rabbi Reinhart visited Glasgow to meet a small group who were also anxious to start a Reform synagogue of their own. West London agreed to pay part of their overheads, and the following year the Glasgow New Synagogue was formally inaugurated. A third London Reform synagogue soon followed, founded by former members of Edgware United Synagogue. Originally known as the Edgware and District Progressive Jewish Fellowship, this became the Edgware and District Reform Synagogue due to the encouragement of Harold Reinhart and his congregation.

The darkening cloud which was now spreading over Europe disturbed Rabbi Reinhart deeply. When the Second World War broke out, and in the years leading up to it, he and Flora concerned themselves tirelessly with the support of the German rabbis who had managed to escape the Nazis. The growing Reform movement urgently needed ministers, and the energy and scholarship of German rabbis, many of whom had attended the celebrated Wissenschaft des Judentums, were most welcome. Many other victims of Nazi Germany also found comfort at Upper Berkeley Street. Refugees were received readily and with affection, and while Harold Reinhart dealt with the problems of the adults, fighting their cause with the Home Office, Flora and her friends founded Lingfield House, a country home for lonely children who had arrived in England without family or possessions. Servicemen and women, on leave in London, could also find a warm welcome and a friendly meal at Seymour Place. Run in the Stern Hall synagogue annexe primarily by a member, Samuel Golden, it was known as The West London Services Club, and was immensely popular with Jews and non-Jews alike. Despite the air raids on London, life there continued much as usual, but the Reinharts had to find temporary accommodation when a bomb damaged their home. The synagogue itself escaped any serious damage, though an incendiary bomb that could have had disastrous results was quickly extinguished on the roof.

After the war, the Reinharts returned to America for a brief holiday, leaving the congregation in the capable hands of its new assistant minister,

Rabbi Curtis Cassell, who lived with his wife and their two young sons in a flat next door to the synagogue in Upper Berkeley Street. Curtis Cassell was one of the young rabbis who had found refuge in England after escaping from Nazi Germany. He had been granted a visa for Australia, but had got only as far as London when war was declared. He was refused a chaplaincy as technically he was an enemy alien, but joined the Pioneer Corps and cheerfully undertook the digging of trenches. His wife, Ceci, with her eight-month old baby, worked as a domestic servant. At the end of the war Rabbi Cassell took up a ministerial post in Glasgow and in 1948 came to West London as assistant minister. He was much loved for his enthusiasm for all things English, ranging from a never-ending supply of jokes to a love of cricket.

The contract of rabbis who worked at the West London Synagogue contained a clause terminating their period of service when they reached the age of 65, though this could be extended by mutual agreement. At 63 Harold Reinhart was as efficient and energetic as he had ever been. In 1954, in the best of health, he celebrated 25 years at Upper Berkeley Street, but certain tensions were emerging in his relationship with the governing body of the synagogue. The chairman, Owen Mocatta, vice-chairman, Leonard Montefiore and treasurers, Edward Henriques and Ralph Pinto, were all influenced by long-established Anglo-Jewish traditions. These were men who served the synagogue and the community loyally and honourably, but did not expect their affiliation to make undue demands on their time or to draw them more closely into Jewish life than they thought necessary. Some correspondence in *The Synagogue Review* of the time on the subject of 'Does a Jew have to attend synagogue to be a good Jew?' brought this issue into prominence.

A more sensitive cause of Rabbi Reinhart's unease arose from his awareness of the increasing commercialism of some aspects of synagogue administration. Differential seat rentals dismayed him, as did any form of discrimination on financial grounds. His outspokenness on this and other aspects of synagogue policy met with considerable resentment. Leonard Montefiore, a close friend of Harold Reinhart, described him thus in a private letter to a member of the council: 'He is opinionated, if not egocentric, blind to anything of value outside B. St., impervious to any notion that we may all make mistakes and life is only possible with compromises and give and take'. Montefiore himself, the only son of Claud Montefiore, though something of a dilettante, was a man of culture and discrimination, a scholar and a wit, loving eccentricity in others and appreciating the good qualities of his friends while tolerant of their foibles. Characteristically he goes on to say of his friend: 'HFR provides what the average Berkeley Streeter of today wants: a fine, dignified building, with dignified services, old and new blended on the High Holydays, acceptable to most worshippers, admirably organised classes, and when needed and asked for, pastoral comfort and sympathy in times of distress. Unfortunately, he is passionately sincere; he really believes when he reads the prayers he is addressing the Almighty; he doesn't believe in mental reservations.'

This was a fair appraisal of Harold Reinhart's nature, and inevitably the continuation of a long and distinguished ministry became the subject of acrimonious debate. 'Who will free me from this turbulent priest?' might well have been echoed by the council, and the opportunity seemed to present itself; why not simply deny the minister the option of continuing in office for some further years? But Harold Reinhart's 'passionate sincerity' was the very quality which endeared him to a great many of his congregation. Members received an invitation to attend a special general meeting on 2 July, 1956, at Friends' House, Euston Road. The main item on the agenda was a resolution proposing 'That in view of his twenty-seven years devoted service to the West London Synagogue, which has so largely contributed to its present reputation and the position it holds as a religious force in the Anglo-Jewish community, and his undoubted capacity to continue such service with unimpaired vigour, the senior minister be invited to remain in office until August 1961 so that a further period may be secured during which our congregation may enjoy the benefit of his spiritual guidance.'

The discussion was inevitably outspoken and at times heated. A ballot of members (for which a special resolution was needed) declared the meeting to be in favour, by a very small majority, of extending Rabbi Reinhart's tenure by another five years. This could hardly be seen as an unequivocal vote of confidence, but did at least give a breathing space for the situation to be re-assessed. However, the five years additional tenure had hardly begun before further disagreements began to make themselves felt. A young minister, Alan Miller, had been employed by the synagogue on a one-year basis, but his appointment as religious education adviser was extended for a further year to 31 July, 1957. Rev. Miller, after attending Oxford and Jews' College and serving briefly as an army chaplain, had helped out with services at S.W. Essex Synagogue. He had now been offered a more lucrative post in a large commercial organisation, but the synagogue council wished to prolong his employment at Upper Berkeley Street. They were confronted with the disapproval of both the Senior Minister and Rabbi Cassell. The reasons for the ministers' disquiet are perhaps difficult to analyse after so many years. No doubt a clash of personalities was involved, but Harold Reinhart, who had been much in favour of Alan Miller's original appointment, was above all perturbed by the council's reluctance to accept his advice on a matter which he felt to be entirely within his province. On 21 March 1957, the council passed a resolution appointing Alan Miller to the post of part-time youth education officer, with effect from 1 August. Rabbi Reinhart and Rabbi Cassell immediately tendered their resignations, to take effect on 31 July.

On 17 May, Owen Mocatta, chairman of the synagogue, died, and his place was taken by a distinguished lawyer, A. S. Diamond, a master in the High Court. The congregation's problems persisted, and another special general meeting of members was called for 17 June at Friends' House. The large hall was packed with members, many of whom were attending a synagogue meeting for the first time. There were three resolutions on the agenda: first, that in view of the resignations of the ministers following the appointment of Alan Miller, that appointment should be rescinded and the ministers invited to withdraw their resignations. Second, that in view of the resignations a committee of enquiry should be set up to investigate the matter. And third, that a way out of the impasse could be found, with goodwill on both sides, by an arrangement under which Mr Miller would act only as visiting lecturer at West London Synagogue. It was a distressing occasion, ending in the confirmation of Alan Miller's appointment and the consequent resignation of Harold Reinhart and Curtis Cassell. The three wardens, Bob Toeman, Lewis Golden and Sam Ansell, also chose to resign, as did the warden elect, Leo Bernard, and, most significantly, the chairman of the education committee, Albert Polack, an educationalist of much experience and unquestioned independence of judgement in such matters.

The ministers wrote to all members of the congregation a few days later, thanking those who had supported them, especially the wardens and the chairman of the education committee, whose resignations had coincided with their own. In this letter they said, 'Members will not believe that any trivial, arbitrary or personal reasons could have induced us to forsake our flock.' On 4 July, the annual general meeting of the synagogue was held at 33 Seymour Place. One resolution read bluntly: 'The wardens, having found it impossible to remain impartial during the recent internal difficulties in synagogue administration and tendered their resignations, be informed forthwith that such resignations be accepted.'

By this time the press, both Jewish and non-Jewish, had become aware of the conflict. *The Jewish Chronicle* quoted from the ministers' letter to the congregation, and summed up the situation as 'least said, soonest mended'. The paper printed a letter signed by Leonard Stein, Frank Waley, A. I. Polack, B. I. Toeman, Lewis Golden, Sam Ansell and Leo Bernard, explaining that 'the ministers acted as they did on grounds of principle, feeling that the disregard of their advice on a matter so clearly within the scope of their responsibilities made it impossible for them to continue to serve the congregation.'

The schism in the synagogue caused much heartache among members. Some families were divided in their loyalties; others, who had been associated with West London for generations, could not bring themselves to make the break, in spite of their respect and affection for Harold Reinhart. Those members who had been involved in synagogue affairs for some time and were aware of the issues involved were hardly surprised by the outcome, but to others the notification of the events came as a shock, as did the finality of the resignations. Many tears were shed over personal problems caused by the departure of much-loved ministers from an apparently stable congregation. Bar-mitzvahs, weddings, funerals and other personal ceremonies were suddenly thrown into question, and members felt troubled and insecure. Rabbi Cassell accepted a position as minister of the Reform congregation in Bulawayo in Southern Rhodesia, leaving London with his family almost at once. *The Synagogue Review* of September 1957 speaks of him with much affection, pointing out that the unobtrusive manner in which he undertook his duties may have concealed his fine qualities.

Harold Reinhart's last sermon at Upper Berkeley Street, on 26 July 1957, told of Jeremiah's denunciation of the priests, the judges, the rulers and the prophets. 'Man,' Rabbi Reinhart said, 'should practise the piety of priesthood, should exercise the justice of the judge, should take the responsibility of a ruler and should serve God as a prophet. The plea of Jeremiah is for those fundamental virtues, the responsibility for which shines forth especially in these high offices, but which lives in every human soul.' The words came from the heart, and it was appropriate that in his beloved Room of Prayer a few days later his last words to his congregation, ended with the priestly blessing: '. . . the Lord lift up his countenance upon you and give you peace.'

CHAPTER II

THE NEW LONDON JEWISH CONGREGATION

When it became clear that events at the West London Synagogue were heading towards a confrontation, those most closely involved thought long and hard of the best way to deal with the crisis. Harold Reinhart himself had much to do in preparing for his departure. The daily responsibility of running the largest Jewish congregation in Britain was demanding, particularly for a man who had long occupied himself with every aspect of its administration. Telephone calls and letters from colleagues, personal friends, members, and the press were time-consuming; anyone who has worked for a large concern for many years and has suddenly to 'clear his desk' will understand such problems. He made it clear to friends who wanted to discuss the future that he was committed to Upper Berkeley Street until 31 July and would not wish to make any firm decisions until that time.

However, this did not deter his closest associates from making plans. Several informal meetings were held during these anxious days, and one in particular, at the home of Doris Herschorn in Portman Square, set the course for the immediate future. It was a private gathering; no minutes were kept, but in the memories of those who were present it represents a crucial step forward. The first public meeting, however, is on record; it was held at the Royal Empire Society in Northumberland Avenue on 16 July. Its purpose was to explore the possibility of forming an altogether new congregation, comprising initially those members who wished to secede from West London and give their allegiance to Rabbi Reinhart, if he would agree to lead them. No-one was asked to enter into any commitment at that stage, nor could the minister be approached until he had officially left his post.

Forty-five people were present at this meeting, including most of those who had resigned their offices at West London. Sir Seymour Karminski, who was in the chair, reviewed the background of the events which had led to the meeting being called, and suggested that it should discuss 'the possibility of forming a new congregation which would serve the purpose of retaining the services of Mr Reinhart as a spiritual leader in Anglo-Jewry and give those who wished for it a religious centre in accordance with their tastes and feelings.' The meeting considered whether a new synagogue might be founded even without Rabbi Reinhart's leadership, especially as the geographical area covered by West London was now so extensive. It was also pointed out that a new congregation might resolve the lack of cohesion and personal contact with ministers that had troubled many at West London. Consideration was given to a waiting period of, say, six months which might allow feelings to cool, and some of those present felt that more might be achieved by remaining at West London in order to exert some influence. The meeting brought back echoes of the schism from which the West London Synagogue itself had emerged in its own early days.

The important questions of burial rights and religious education were discussed and the approaching High Holydays were much in mind, but these were only a part of the concerns those present felt about the future. After an open and frank debate, Sir Seymour put the following resolution to the meeting: That a new congregation be formed under the auspices of the Association of Synagogues in Great Britain and with the support and leadership of Rabbi Reinhart. It was carried by a show of hands and a committee was immediately elected. Sir Seymour declined to serve as the new chairman on account of the pressure of his own work, and the committee agreed to elect one at their first meeting.

It was agreed that during the remainder of the summer and the period of the High Holydays the committee would establish the main structure of the new congregation, and would invite those who had already expressed interest to an inaugural meeting later in the year. Notices were sent out during August under the name of The New London Jewish Congregation – a temporary name chosen by the committee – to all those who attended the

2. *Rabbi Harold Reinhart, the first minister of the congregation*

meeting at the Royal Empire Society, inviting them to apply for tickets to High Holyday services to be held at the Rudolph Steiner Hall, near Baker Street. In the event, these services, led by Rabbi Reinhart, were attended by some 300 people. Until the formal inauguration, the committee (now the council) consisted of Frank Waley, as chairman, Albert Polack as vice-chairman, Lewis Golden as treasurer and Pat Reigate and Constance Stuart as joint honorary secretaries.

Frank Waley was the son of the Philip Waley who had brought Rabbi Reinhart over from America in 1929. Frank, an officer in the Prince of Wales Own South Lancashire Regiment, had been wounded in the First World War, earning both a Military Cross and a limp, which remained with him for the rest of his life. His gruff manner concealed a great affection for the Reinharts and a wicked sense of humour. He always enjoyed telling the story of a young Jewish private under his command, sent to peel potatoes in the canteen. He was discovered later scribbling poems on bits of paper which were immediately consigned to the fire. Thus Frank lost the opportunity of owning the manuscripts of some of Isaac Rosenberg's fine war poems. Frank was a distinguished gardener, judging at the Chelsea Flower Show and prepared to trek through the mountains of Turkey and Portugal in search of rare specimens of the tiny daffodils and wild cyclamen which he loved. His other passion was for trees, and he was awarded the OBE for services to arboriculture. Every year members of the congregation would drive down to his garden at Sevenoaks to bring back greenery to decorate the Succah. Never a very observant Jew, Frank always came to the synagogue on the Day of Atonement, where he read the book of Jonah in his husky old-Etonian voice, making up in sincerity what was lost in clarity. His synagogue and his garden were the two great loves of his life and he served both tirelessly to the end of his days. The armorial family motto, granted to the Waleys by King William IV in 1834, was Fortiter et Fideliter – Bravely and Faithfully.

The other members of the council were Sam Ansell, Leo Bernard, Margaret Blumenthal, Sidney Craft, Doris Herschorn, Susan Karminski,

Ivan Marre, Harry Reigate, Arthur Tasher and Bob Toeman. They subsequently elected Sir Seymour Karminski as president, Bob Toeman, Sam Ansell and Lewis Golden as wardens and Betty Polack as an additional member of the council.

There was much to be done. Caxton Hall was chosen as a suitable location for Sabbath and festival services. Later to be converted into flats, the building was at that time widely known as London's principal registry office and the fashionable place for society weddings. Frequently congregants on a Sabbath morning had to fight their way through swathes of press photographers and showers of confetti. The hall also offered a meeting place for more than one eccentric organisation. Synagogue services were often held in a room adjacent to The Aetherius Society, whose directives were believed to emanate from Outer Space. The administrators of Caxton Hall became good friends of the congregation, helpfully providing storage space for the temporary Ark and meeting other needs. This Ark had been designed by Rabbi Reinhart, and those who arrived early for services frequently found him setting it up himself and putting out the chairs; no task was ever beneath his dignity. When a permanent home was later found the manager of Caxton Hall was a welcome guest at the opening service.

The new project made good progress. Harold Reinhart had undertaken to lead the congregation in an honorary capacity; in fact during the whole of his service to the congregation he never received payment, although it later became possible to provide the Reinharts with a rent free flat at Kent House. He and Flora derived much encouragement from the spirit of the group. In his first letter to members, dated 31 December 1957, after the inaugural meeting, he wrote: 'I am writing to express to you my gratification over the progress of our effort. It is five months since July 1957 when the founding of our congregation was first suggested. It is three months since, on Rosh Hashanah 5718 we began the conduct of divine services. It is two months since our congregation was formally organised. In this short time, faith, counsel, prayer and fellowship have achieved more than any one of us could have expected – not so much in what it shows outwardly, as in our own minds' assurance that we possess something real, precious and enduring . . . In this naughty and confused world I have never been party to an undertaking which, modest though it is, is yet so soundly dictated by high principle . . . I began this letter with an expression of gratitude for friendship. Let me end with a profession of devotion to truth. We are seeking a refuge from evasion, pretence and time-serving, which are rife everywhere and which mercilessly beguile religious societies. The rock upon which we are resolved to build is loyalty to our cause, truth to one another, honesty with ourselves, faith in the Eye which never sleeps. We will make a synagogue which will stand as a challenge to the best in each of us, and in which membership will be a happy burden and a precious privilege to us all. I prize the confidence in my efforts which you have so generously shown, and I honour your every service to dig a new pure channel for the living fountain of our ancient faith.'

One of the earliest communal events, still recalled with pleasure by several of those present, was the first Succah. Located in the garden of the St John's Wood home of Bob and Iris Toeman, the temporary construction was filled with flowers and fruit in an original and elegant design, and as Mr Reinhart said, provided 'a delight to the eye and a stimulus to the imagination'. The infant congregation received help from many quarters. Prayer books, until they could be purchased, were courteously loaned by West London; two Sifre Torah were presented, and all those involved worked tirelessly to ensure the smooth running of an organisation that was in some respects unique.

One invaluable member, then and for many years to come, was Constance Stuart. She came from a Scottish Presbyterian family, and may well have been a direct descendant of Mary Stuart, Mary Queen of Scots (woe betide anyone who spelt her name 'Stewart'). Many years earlier she had become engaged to a young French Jew who, with his family, had been taken by the Nazis. Always reticent about herself, Constance never revealed why she had turned to Harold Reinhart for support, but she became a Jewess with full formality (he was one of her sponsors) and devoted herself from then on to the welfare of the synagogue and of the Reinharts. The women in the Stuart family were all highly intelligent and strong-minded. Her mother had been a suffragette and her sister the headmistress of a girls' school. After leaving school Constance worked as a shorthand-typist at Touche, Ross & Co., where she trained as an accountant, and was the first woman to qualify as a chartered secretary. She remained with Touche's until she retired, learning to appreciate fine wine and visiting France with Sir George Touche to learn about medieval church architecture. Later she persuaded Touche's, one of the leading international accountancy firms, to give generous help to a small congregation of London Jews! After she retired Constance moved to Aldeburgh where she played an important part in the affairs of the town and its music festival, welcoming many members of the congregation as her guests. She died there recently, and is much missed.

It was now possible to put the establishment of the synagogue on a formal footing. An inaugural general meeting was called for 29 October 1957 at the Kensington Palace Hotel. Sir Seymour and Lady Karminski welcomed those present at a reception, and this was followed by the meeting – about 150 people were present – with Sir Seymour in the chair. Until that stage, no-one had been called upon to enter into any commitment, but the hard work of the council had now produced a constitution, together with a scale of subscriptions. Those present were invited to sign the original document of constitution as founder members, and Rabbi Reinhart and the honorary officers were confirmed in office. The subscription for a husband and wife where the husband was aged 30 or over was set at £26.5.0. per annum, a not inconsiderable sum in those days, though of course with no additional charges for seats.

The preliminary constitution confirmed the name of the congregation and stated that its objects were 'to provide a centre for Jewish worship and study, and to further religious and charitable undertakings appropriate to such a centre.' Provision was to be made for weddings, funerals and other Jewish ceremonies such as bar- and bat-mitzvahs, and for a Junior Membership. During the following August a general meeting would be held to adopt such laws as were deemed necessary for the conduct of the synagogue.

During the congregation's first year services were held regularly at Caxton Hall or at a nearby hotel when Caxton Hall was closed. All the festivals were observed: Hanucah, Purim, Pesach – with a communal Seder – Shavuot, the High Holydays, and Succot. Provision of music for the services was not easy. However, a piano was available and Mrs Lily Ball accompanied a voluntary choir. Rabbi Reinhart reported, 'We attempt congregational singing – we are attempting the impossible – we are hopeful of success.' A young Israeli pianist, Gideon Shamir, helped out with the music. Rabbi Reinhart wrote at that time to another young musician inviting him to provide music for the services, but the recipient of the letter left it on his mantlepiece for nearly a year. Then he re-read it and telephoned Harold Reinhart, apologising for his neglect. 'Do you still need a pianist for your services?' he asked. 'We do indeed,' was the reply, and thus Harold Lester joined the congregation which he has served so generously for some forty-five years, as organist, accompanist, chazan, Purim entertainer and in many other ways. His services to the synagogue have been combined with a distinguished career in the world of music, with special distinction as a player of the harpsichord. Later, the congregation was no less indebted to Raymond Fischer for his contribution to synagogue life both as a musician and in other capacities.

Although the early services at Caxton Hall were simple and the congregation had few possessions, the generosity of friends soon led to gifts of accoutrements for the Torah scrolls, help with the necessities of synagogue life, and, when necessary, assistance with the services themselves. Several distinguished guest preachers gave sermons, children's classes were soon under way and the number of babies blessed in front of the Holy Ark showed a determination to ensure that the congregation would continue from generation to generation! The first wedding at Caxton Hall, was, most appropriately, that of the chairman's daughter, Rosemary Waley, to John Sassoon.

However, the matter that occupied the minds of members of the council above all others was the search for a permanent home and a location committee had been set up under the chairmanship of Lady Karminski. Its challenging task was to find a house or hall, centrally situated, suitable for use as a synagogue, and with rooms for meetings, offices and classrooms. Rabbi Reinhart made it very clear in his monthly letters to members that it was the spirit of the congregation that mattered most, rather than an imposing home, and when it was suggested to him that this approach might discourage new members, he replied, 'We are a small group and we hope to grow. But not at any price. Size itself is no advantage; the dinosaur was the largest of beasts.'

Harold Reinhart was a demanding leader, demanding of himself as well as of his congregation. His convictions extended to secular matters and he was never afraid to declare them. He was an active member of The Jewish Peace Society, where he served on the committee alongside the Chief Rabbi, Israel Brodie. He spoke forcefully in favour of the abolition of capital punishment, and reprinted in one letter to members the national appeal of the Campaign for Nuclear Disarmament. Many of his congregants complained ruefully that they could 'never say no' to Harold Reinhart, but his own vigour and his enthusiasm for his new congregation swept him onward. It was frequently suggested by his critics that he was opposed to Zionism. He had indeed always declined to include a prayer for Israel in the Sabbath service, as he felt that it was inappropriate; but there is no doubt that the welfare of the state of Israel lay close to his heart. On the 10th anniversary of the founding of the state he quoted to his congregants the words of Robert Carvalho, the president of the Anglo-Jewish Association: 'We regard ourselves as loyal British citizens and see no conflict in also having the greatest interest and fellowship with our brothers in Israel.' Rabbi Reinhart continued, 'It is, I believe, in this spirit that at this time of their tenth anniversary we fervently wish our brethren in the State of Israel progress towards a just peace with their neighbours, and rich opportunity to develop their national life for the good of many and the hurt of none.'

News from Rabbi Cassell in Bulawayo and visits from colleagues kept the New London Jewish Congregation in touch with old friends, and when Henry de Metz, for many years West London's highly regarded beadle, died, it was Harold Reinhart who conducted the funeral.

By October the congregation had been in existence for a year. The second Succah was as exciting and unusual as the first. By permission of the ambassador, Eliahu Elath, who had become a personal friend of Rabbi Reinhart, it was held in the gardens of the Israeli Embassy in Palace Green. It was, once again, in a rare and beautiful setting, and the ladies responsible for its decoration were able to come and go as they wished, through the gate in the wall beside the fire station, with little thought in those days for security concerns. A month later the congregation held its first annual general meeting. Rabbi Reinhart spoke of his satisfaction at what had been achieved, and was thanked by the president for his freely-given leadership and hard work during the year. The treasurer in turn was congratulated on a surplus of £2 in the accounts! At a council meeting immediately before this a resolution had been passed which was to cause much controversy in the congregation. It had been resolved that the age for bar- and bat-mitzvah should be set at sixteen years. This policy continued to be a cause of debate for many years to come, despite forceful advocacy by Rabbi Reinhart. Although it was applied with some flexibility it resulted on more than one occasion in the resignation of members.

The hunt for a suitable synagogue proved a difficult task. At the suggestion of Constance Stuart, a building fund had been set up and had accumulated a considerable sum, which was to prove vital when a building was eventually found. The location committee favoured an area south of Hyde Park and in the City of Westminster. At the second annual general meeting on 19 January 1960 the honorary treasurer was able to report to members that the surplus in the accounts was due mainly to the fact that the minister served in an honorary capacity. He told the meeting that the location committee had found a building in Rutland Gardens, Knightsbridge, opposite the barracks, which seemed to be ideally suited as a home for the congregation. It was hoped that it would be possible to purchase the freehold and make the necessary alterations in order to convert it into a synagogue. Its name was Kent House and a full account of its remarkable history will be found later in this book.

CHAPTER III

A NEW HOME

The search for a permanent home had been much in the minds of the minister and the congregation. Harold Reinhart, a lover of poetry and himself a poet of some merit, would often include one of his own poems in his monthly letter. In November 1959, clearly preoccupied with the homelessness of his followers, he offered a dialogue between The Synagogue and The Jew. The first two verses epitomised his spirit:

The Synagogue: I need you, Jew, your heartbeat and your breathing;
I need your work and woe; I need your laughter;
I need your loyalty and your commitment;
I need your life; in you I have my being.
The Jew: I need you, Synagogue,
A dwelling for my soul ;
My past, my future hope,
My individual distinct humanity.

In the meantime congregational life continued with enthusiasm. The members held a reception at Caxton Hall to welcome Rabbi and Mrs Hugo Gryn back from a stay in India and hear something of their experiences. The annual Festivals were all celebrated with enjoyment, and the High Holydays brought many newcomers to participate in the services. But house-hunting remained a pressing concern. In August 1958 the location committee had formally invited the estate agents D. E. and J. Levy to find premises for the synagogue. Several unsuitable buildings were suggested, as well as two vacant sites. However the committee felt that a purpose-built synagogue would prove too costly. A site in Rutland Gate, suggested by a member of the congregation with property experience, seemed a possibility, but it was unlikely that planning permission would be granted. Kent House, a large building in Rutland Gardens, was more promising. Its tenants, Telephone Rentals Ltd., did not wish to renew their lease, and D. E. and J. Levy were accordingly asked by the committee to examine the building. Their report described the house as containing 'magnificent rooms with decorative ceilings, arranged as two large halls, five reception rooms, fifteen bedrooms and four bathrooms.' The first offer from the synagogue was not acceptable, and the agents suggested instead an old warehouse in Covent Garden. The committee persisted, won over by the splendour of the house, and finally agreed a mutually acceptable price. This was not quite the end of the matter, for Levy's put in a bill for commission on the purchase of a house which had in fact been found by the congregation without their help! With Constance Stuart's firm handling, the matter was brought to an amicable conclusion.

On 28 February 1960 a special general meeting was held at St James's Court, opposite Caxton Hall. The president, Sir Seymour Karminski, was in the chair. The meeting was asked to pass a resolution 'That the agreement entered into with Mr R. C. Yablon by Mr L. L. Golden on behalf of himself and all other members on 10 February 1960, relating to the congregation's purchase of Kent House, Knightsbridge, be and is hereby approved.' The operation of the agreement was dependent upon the granting of bank overdraft facilities, which in turn required the congregation to find guarantors for a balance of £10,000 not covered by the agreement. Ralph Yablon, always generous as far as the congregation was concerned, offered to three members the opportunity of investing in a company which might later be quoted on the stock exchange. These shares enabled bank overdrafts to be obtained, and although the members concerned were at some risk in thus helping the synagogue, all went well. The investment soon paid off and the gain on the sale of the shares was then used to repay a large part of the synagogue's own overdraft. The meeting warmly congratulated Lady Karminski and her committee, and, of course Ralph Yablon, whose involvement and generosity were to be of incalculable benefit to the synagogue on many occasions. Congratulations were certainly well deserved: the committee was about to acquire a large, handsome, four-storeyed freehold building in an excellent location for the finally agreed price of £83,000.

On 7th April a brief note appeared in the Minister's letter:

IT'S OURS!!

Yesterday, the purchase of Kent House, Rutland Gardens, Knightsbridge, was completed on behalf of the congregation. I congratulate every member. Let us each breathe a prayer of fervent thanks that we have reached this stage,

3. *The exterior of Kent House*

and a most earnest petition to Heaven for light and strength to meet the challenge that awaits us.

A few weeks later another general meeting was called so that members could hear formally of the completion of the purchase. The building was bought in the name of Lanimon Properties Ltd. (later to be changed to Kent House, Knightsbridge Ltd.), a company wholly owned by the congregation. At this meeting a second most important decision was taken: the name of the congregation was to be changed to The Westminster Synagogue. Other names, such as the Knightsbridge Synagogue, had been suggested, but 'Westminster' was strongly supported. There was no other active Jewish congregation in the City of Westminster, though a small synagogue in Soho did use a transliterated form of the name in Hebrew. Rabbi Reinhart's usual diplomatic skill overcame all objections. The word 'The' was originally included in the title but was later dropped to leave simply Westminster Synagogue, a fitting name in a historic part of London. The purchase of the house was duly reported in the Jewish and national press.

At the time of the purchase much of the house was in poor condition. The war-time tenants had not always been considerate; for example, holes had been dug in the fine marble flooring to erect office partitions. The wiring was in poor state, as were the heating and the plumbing, and a considerable amount of redecoration was needed before the house could be used by the congregation. The building committee, under the chairmanship of Sam Ansell, felt that the congregation should move in at the earliest possible moment, even if sufficient funds were not available for a full refurbishment. The best course, it was felt, would be to complete the essential work in the basement and on the ground floor; this would mean that the sanctuary could occupy the large Rutland room, whilst the main offices, including the rabbi's study, would be in the Knightsbridge room; a caretaker's flat could be prepared in the rooms beyond the kitchen.

As the summer passed, the work at Kent House continued, with many members helping in the refurbishment and many friends offering gifts. Among the most welcome was a contribution from J. Samuel & Son, the

4. *The Holy Ark, formerly the fireplace of the dining room at Kent House*

well-known monumental stonemasons, who had always respected Rabbi Reinhart from their association with him on many sad occasions in the past. They designed and presented to the synagogue the two white panels on which were inscribed Hebrew verses, and into which were set two wall-lights, and later, when the congregation moved to the first floor, the black and gold plaques on which are engraved the opening words of the Ten Commandments, and which hang on either side of the Holy Ark. Louis M. Samuel, managing director of J. Samuel & Son, had worked as a young apprentice mason in Westminster Abbey and at Westminster Cathedral, and his high regard for Harold Reinhart led him to add Westminster Synagogue to his credentials. Other members and friends wore out their knees and their fingers cleaning, polishing and scrubbing, under the active leadership of the Reinharts. Flora was to be seen blackleading the grates and fireplaces, while Harold climbed ladders to instal lamps and hang curtains. No casualties were reported, perhaps by good fortune rather than by good management.

The general colour scheme was not unlike that used sixty years earlier by Celia and Saxton Noble during their occupation of the house: warm tones of russet, chestnut and gold harmonised with the ceiling cornices, carpets, curtains and ark fabrics, giving a restrained beauty to the whole synagogue. There were inevitably some heated debates about the furnishings and fittings; Gertrude Nathan, Frank Waley's sister, recalls 'an awful tussle with the purple and crimson brigade'. One particular triumph was the purchase of some 200 comfortable chairs, imported from Eastern Europe at a cost of about £2 each; in spite of constant use, the majority have lasted to this day.

On 11 August 1960, Harold Reinhart wrote to the congregation 'in affection, gratitude and hope' to inform them that their new home was ready. The inaugural service was to take place on the Sabbath morning of 17 September. Arrangements for this grand occasion were impressive. The music was in the able hands of Harold Lester and a large congregation filled the Rutland room and overflowed into the Marble Hall. The room looked splendid, a revelation to those who had not seen it or had been sceptical of its possibilities. Flowers were abundant and there was an atmosphere of excited anticipation. The wardens, in full morning dress and top hats, as was the custom in the early years of the congregation, were Sam Ansell, Leo Bernard and Sidney Craft. Little David Golden, the treasurer's son, pulled

5A. *The first wedding at Kent House, 1960, of Ezra Dingoor to Eileen Parker*

a cord to reveal the Ner Tamid, which remains one of the few in a London synagogue to burn oil rather than electricity. Rabbi Michael Curtis, secretary to the Beth Din of the Association of Synagogues in Great Britain and a good friend to the synagogue, read from the scroll. Rabbi Reinhart's heartfelt sermon left many in the congregation near to tears. He spoke of the early beginnings of the synagogue, and the 'high enterprise' on which it was engaged. 'A true synagogue', he said, 'had to be a source of stimulus, guidance and solace.' Those present were moved by his words, aware of the difficult decisions some of them had made to be there. In the Knightsbridge room after the service, Albert Polack welcomed the guests.

'A.I.', as he was known to generations of Jewish boys and their parents, had taken over Polack's House at Clifton College from his uncle Philip (he was to hand it on in turn to his son, Ernest). There, with his wife Betty, he had not only given the boys in his charge a sense of pride in their Jewish identity, but had also instilled, like the best of traditional schoolmasters, a love of the classics and of the English language and its literature. He served for many years as the education officer of the Council of Christians and Jews, and

5B. *The Ner Tamid above the Holy Ark*

few would forget his upright integrity. At Westminster Synagogue A. I. gave sermons, conducted meetings and guided the congregation, always in his beautifully modulated voice and gentlemanly manner. At this reception Rabbi Reinhart was presented with a copy of Augustus Hare's *Walks in London*, which mentions Kent House, and recalled in his words of thanks the workmen who had refurbished the building (sadly their foreman had died in the course of the work). He read messages from Rabbi Cassell and from others who could not be present. All who were there will long have remembered that morning.

Once the congregation was established in its own home, the house was quickly put to full use. Children's parties at Hanucah, a young people's group, and visiting societies, as well as baby-blessings, bar-mitzvahs and bat-mitzvahs and marriages gave the building life and excitement. The first wedding at Kent House was that of Eileen Shoshana Parker to Ezra Solomon Dingoor; forty years later both Eileen and Ezra were still playing an active part in the running of the synagogue. A suitable place had been found for a Succah, and each year this was decked with great swathes of greenery from Frank Waley's garden in Sevenoaks.

In its early days at Kent House the congregation acquired the services of a man who was to play for many years a vital role in keeping the building – and the congregation – in perfect running order. Cecil Bradley, the caretaker, was the epitome of a discreet, efficient but kindly butler; in fact he had served for a while as 'a gentleman's gentleman'. He liked to tell of his first interview at Kent House. The door was opened to him by Rabbi Reinhart in his shirtsleeves. Hardly had he stepped over the threshold when he was asked to hold some wood steady for the rabbi's carpentry efforts. They became friends at once. He knew most of the congregation by name and maintained very high standards of care in the house. He was always known only as Mr Bradley, and visitors who behaved brashly or self-importantly he deemed to be 'not quite our sort'. He had acquired his knowledge of the Jewish community from a previous post at Norwood Orphanage, but he remained a very private person and the synagogue was his whole existence for some thirty years. He cleaned and polished, prepared the sanctuary for services, attending to all the needs of the minister and the congregation. He would exchange a joke or two with those he knew well but no unseemly words ever passed his lips. He did once introduce a cat into his private flat but it was seldom visible, and after it had once made its way across the floor of the synagogue (fortunately not on a Sabbath morning) it disappeared and was never seen again. He was closely associated with St Paul's Cathedral, and seemed to have no difficulty in sharing his affections between the cathedral and the synagogue. Mr Bradley served the congregation for some three decades until his retirement to Eastbourne. He died on 23 April 1992, the birthday of William Shakespeare and also St George's Day. He would have found that appropriate.

The third annual general meeting, the first at Kent House, was remarkably well attended. About half the members were present, perhaps a record for a religious institution. It was at this meeting that the congregation approved unanimously a document which can have had few parallels in contemporary Jewish life. This was the 'Statement of Principles and Policy'. Rabbi Reinhart and a number of members had long wished to formulate the aims and principles of the congregation, with particular reference to the priorities which had led to its foundation. The statement has since appeared every year as an introduction to the annual report and accounts. It reads as follows:

PRINCIPLES

Our aim is to create a synagogue which will be an instrument for the pursuit of religious truth. We would seek for knowledge and charity and piety. We want a congregation which will be a source of encouragement to human progress and of comfort and inspiration to individual men and women. We would be a congregation of interested active members, personally committed to our synagogue, accepting the responsibility of membership as a challenge to the best in each of us. We regard our membership as a high privilege, and we will not be content with a synagogue which is less than a vehicle of truth.

POLICY

For the realisation of our aims, we deem it essential that our synagogue should be the centre of a Holy Congregation of men and women believing in Judaism as a relevant motivating power in their lives. Through our synagogue we should participate in the life of Jewry as a whole, and in human endeavour in the wider community.

We believe that such a synagogue should be a democratic society in which practice and procedure are determined by the members themselves, and we are conscious of a sense of congregational responsibility to interpret courageously our heritage and to adventure in our religious expression. In our services we strive to give voice to the authentic tradition expressed in a manner suitable to our times.

Our membership subscription is set at a figure which we consider realistic in the contemporary world, and appropriate for a seriously interested person of moderate means. Members are asked to bear a proper share of the necessary expense of maintaining a synagogue. Some will be able to pay more, others less. The amount itself is not important – significance lies in the token of seriousness, of commitment.

We would avoid commercialism in our congregational management. While we appreciate the need to direct our affairs in a businesslike manner, we are determined that our congregation shall not be conducted as a business, that no services or privileges shall be bought or paid for, and that all members shall have precisely the same rights, duties and responsibilities.

We offer our services to all who wish for them, in the belief that the more we give, the more we shall ourselves possess. It may then be asked if our services are available to all people, why become a member? Our answer is that membership signifies personal participation in a dedicated effort to safeguard our Jewish tradition and serve our Jewish ideal.

We know that a true synagogue is one in which the members participate in congregational prayer and study, and maintain a humane administration. We attest our need for such a synagogue and our will to achieve it.

The enthusiasm of the early years was evident in a very active congregation. Numbers by this fourth year had considerably increased, and many members played some part in the affairs of the synagogue. Sunday classes for the children were well attended, and all celebrations and congregational events were handled by the members themselves. The arranging of the communal Seder was the especial prerogative of Flora Reinhart, who guided her willing helpers with a firm hand. One story, apocryphal no doubt, has her on hands and knees measuring the height of the tablecloths above the floor to see that all were the same. These occasions brought into use a particularly generous gift from an old friend of the Reinharts, who had presented the synagogue with sixty complete sets of silver cutlery – enough for as many Seder guests as could be accommodated in the Rutland room. The sets were wrapped in individual felt bags and continue to be used on all suitable occasions. They are kept in the huge safe in the kitchen – a legacy

6. *Flora Reinhart*

from the nineteenth century occupants of the house. The kitchen at Kent House was itself something of an antique. It still contains the old floor-to-ceiling wooden cupboards, and the large central table. The great wooden plate rack which stretched across the double stone sinks has now been replaced and the sinks are of stainless steel, but generally it is not difficult to imagine five-course dinners for twenty or more guests being prepared by a staff of servants.

As the congregation settled into its new home, the council was making plans to bring the rest of the building into use. A considerable investment would be needed to make possible the move to the first floor where the synagogue could occupy a larger room. Individual members organised fund-raising activities in their own homes and the building fund committee arranged a dinner dance at the Normandie Hotel. This was very successful, with entertainment by Ron Moody, a tombola and raffle, Scottish dancing and a fine brochure. Congratulating all those concerned, Rabbi Reinhart singled out especially Ivor and Claire Connick 'whose enterprise and energy and happy and gracious spirit were so amply rewarded'. The building fund benefited by £1,650, a substantial sum in those days.

Many other activities now took place at Kent House. An adult group met regularly to study Hebrew; the Young People's Group met on Sunday afternoons, and almost every month the activities committee arranged a lecture, debate or concert, all of which were well attended. Many visitors came to the services and on occasion Rabbi Reinhart had to remind them that the few minutes before the service began, while the organ played, were intended for silent prayer, though it should be said that one look from Mrs Reinhart was enough to bring the message home.

In March 1962 the congregation enjoyed the first of many traditional Purim entertainments. Peter Blom and Harold Lester presented 'Purimpromptu, or At The Drop of a Yarmulka'. Peter's lively sense of humour had become a by-word in synagogue affairs, and his bulky person contrasted with the slender figure of his beautiful wife Cynthia. His wit was of a professional standard and with Harold Lester well able at the piano to enhance anything he wrote, the pair provided memorable entertainment. No-one was immune from their satire, but nor was anyone wounded by it. After that first performance members made sure of their Purim seats in very good time, for the audience flowed out of the Rutland room into the Marble Hall on each occasion. These 'Purimspiels' continued for many years, each seeming to improve on the last. Later, when Peter Blom was no longer active in the congregation, other players and satirists took on his mantle, but Harold Lester has continued to this day to present a virtuoso performance to an enthusiastic audience.

In July 1961 Harold Reinhart reached his 70th birthday. The occasion was celebrated by the congregation a little later so that more members could be present. On Sunday, 1 October many members and friends enjoyed a party at Kent House. A cake in the shape of a book, with Rabbi Reinhart's initials, was an appropriate gesture, as the congregation had decided to mark the birthday by the foundation of a library in his name. The first books acquired for the Reinhart Library and presented on that occasion were the twelve volumes of the new edition of the Soncino Talmud. Some 140 people were present, including representatives of several orthodox and progressive synagogues, and from senior citizens to babes in arms. Writing to thank members Rabbi Reinhart mentioned in particular 'the spontaneity, the genuineness of the spirit of the party, which cheered our hearts because of your friendship, and drew us all closer together in devotion to our common cause.'

CHAPTER IV

THE NEXT STAGE

The greatest problem now facing the congregation was lack of space. Due to flourishing growth and enthusiasm, the ground floor at Kent House was hardly large enough to hold all those who wished to attend Sabbath services, and even less adequate for festivals and the High Holydays; nor were there proper amenities for the rabbi, the synagogue offices and the rapidly growing children's classes. The 1962 High Holydays necessitated careful improvisation. It was generally agreed that no rooms outside Kent House should be used for the services, and the congregation was asked to be patient with temporary arrangements. Two separate rooms were put to use – the synagogue itself and the Knightsbridge room – with the Marble Hall between them. Sound systems were used for the first time, with parts of the service read from different positions, in order to form a unified room of prayer, and the scrolls were carried round the whole congregation.

These arrangements were accepted without complaint, but the council was well aware that by the autumn of the following year the space available to the congregation had to be considerably greater. Plans had also been made to bring the top floor of the building into use as a flat for the minister and his wife, and to consider the possibility of an assistant for him and a paid secretary; the rapidly rising running costs of the synagogue had also to be considered. The bank overdraft had been repaid, and by July, the fifth anniversary of the founding of the synagogue, Rabbi Reinhart was able to congratulate the members on having achieved so much. However, what had been achieved was not quite sufficient to allow for services to be held upstairs; that was promised for the following year, and with a grand dinner dance, other fund-raising activities and many generous donations, the necessary finance was secured.

The congregation and its minister were now playing an active part in the world beyond Rutland Gardens. Rabbi Reinhart, always keenly aware of the problems of the wider community, continued to occupy himself with the difficulties confronting the nation. He spoke at meetings of the Peace Society, of the Campaign for Nuclear Disarmament, at other synagogues, at churches and at public meetings. On occasion he was too hard-pressed to attend to his monthly letter to members and sent a little note of apology instead. The synagogue itself adopted an Indian village – Peddalebaka – and helped to support it. Many distinguished preachers spoke from the Kent House pulpit, among them rabbis of the ASGB, Rabbi Jacob Petuchowski – a former pupil of Rabbi Reinhart on a visit from America – Rabbi Lionel Blue, Rabbi John Rayner and on occasion members of the congregation such as Albert Polack and Leo Bernard.

One notable synagogue activity was inaugurated in 1963. The first Shavuot supper was held at Kent House after the evening service and has since remained an important part of the synagogue calendar. The first speaker was Leonard Stein, OBE, who with his wife Kitty was a founder member of Westminster Synagogue. On this occasion this distinguished colleague of Chaim Weizmann, and author of an important study of the Balfour Declaration, spoke about the history and significance of the Shavuot festival. This began a tradition marked every year by a speaker of distinction, after an excellent supper prepared by the ladies of the congregation.

It was a characteristic decision on the part of the members to dispense with a ladies guild; the women in particular felt that all synagogue activities should be open to every member. This was to some extent a heritage from the earliest days of Reform Judaism when men and women sat together in the synagogue. Nevertheless it was an unusual step; even the Progressive community had been slow to take up the feminist point of view. At Westminster, however, women read from the Torah in the synagogue, took the chair of committees and in later years served as wardens; at the time of writing the synagogue has a woman president. Many of the women members were young professionals who felt that if there was work to be done – arranging meals, decorating the house, caring for the children – they would participate happily. But to meet simply for social reasons was not to their liking, not least because they were widely spread around London. It should be added that many a male member of the congregation donned an apron and helped with the domestic chores.

By the autumn of 1963 the long months of restoration, rebuilding and decoration were coming to an end. The cost – £21,000 – seems today remarkably modest. It included the installation of a lift, the conversion of the large rooms upstairs, refurbishment of the staircase and the furnishing of the whole area. The treasurer, Lewis Golden, with Constance Stuart and Leo Bernard, undertook much of the demanding work of overseeing the move, together with the architect, Thomas Pan, who skilfully designed the central area of the sanctuary. The money was largely borrowed from the bank, with suitable guarantees. The service of thanksgiving and dedication was fixed for a Sunday afternoon, 15 September, and Harold and Flora Reinhart returned on the Queen Mary from a holiday in America in good time for the service. In his absence members of the congregation, assisted on occasion by his colleagues, had taken the synagogue services, an experience which stood them in good stead at a later time when the congregation was without a minister for many months.

Three years, almost to the day, after the first service at Kent House, Westminster Synagogue moved upstairs. A beautiful autumn afternoon enhanced the occasion and the room looked splendid. The great black and gold Ark, formerly the fireplace in the dining-room downstairs, had been extracted from its original place and taken upstairs, where it seemed as if it had always stood. The service proceeded impressively; Albert Polack conducted the first part with the music in Harold Lester's care, with Marta Shelley and Esther Salaman leading the singing. Esther Salaman Hamburger was the daughter of distinguished parents. Her mother, Nina Salaman, was herself a gifted poet as well as a translator of medieval Jewish poetry

7. Cover for a Torah scroll used on the High Holy Days. It was embroidered by Beryl Dean, the ecclesiastical embroiderer, to a design by Harold Reinhart, and is of ecru silk bordered with D'Alencon lace. It is illustrated in Embroideries for Synagogue and Home *by Lillian S. Freehof and Bucky King, 1966.*

and other literature. Her father, Redcliffe Salaman, was a geneticist whose magnum opus, *The History and Social Influence of the Potato*, has remained in print since it was first published in 1949. Esther had a musical training and although brought up in an orthodox background, found the atmosphere congenial at Upper Berkeley Street, where she sang at communal seders. At Caxton Hall she participated in the music of the services. Although a committed member, she was among those who doubted whether the move to Kent House was quite the right one for the synagogue. The house, she felt, was too grand for a modest congregation, but she remained loyal to the minister and to the members, and continued to play an important part in synagogue life. Esther's sister, Ruth Collett, was also a member; she was a distinguished artist, and produced for the synagogue's communal Seders some delightful name-cards, as well as other illustrated work for the children of the congregation.

Many members of the congregation, young and old, took part; the Ner Tamid, brought upstairs to its customary place above the Holy Ark, was lit by the Connick twins, David and Lesley, and in a special prayer those present gave thanks for 'the spark within us that fired us with the desire for this house, and kindled the will to undertake its realisation.' At a reception downstairs following the service, the guests included the Lord Mayor and Lady Mayoress of Westminster, the local Member of Parliament, Sir Harry Hylton-Foster, Q.C., then the Speaker of the House of Commons, distinguished rabbis from almost every section of the Jewish community, as well as representatives of many people who had been involved in the building work (including the bank manager!) and visitors from Jewish and non-Jewish organisations. Words of thanks and congratulations followed the excellent tea, and there were warm messages of encouragement from those who could not be present.

In February 1965 the congregation embarked on a project of great significance both for Westminster Synagogue and for the wider community. On a cold grey morning two large lorries eased their way into Rutland

Gardens. There to witness the dramatic arrival of 1,564 Sifre Torah from Czechoslovakia were Rabbi Reinhart, several members of the congregation, and press and television representatives. During the Nazi occupation of the provinces of Moravia and Bohemia, when countless Jews were killed and their synagogues burned, these scrolls of the law were removed and stored near Prague. The motives of the Nazi occupiers in taking this course are, to this day, unclear. It is thought possible that they envisaged some kind of exhibition of a defunct race, but it has also been suggested that when the synagogues were destroyed, some tremor of superstition stayed their hand. At all events, the scrolls survived, and at the end of the war were rescued through the good offices of Erik Estorick, a London art dealer, with a generous endowment from a member of the congregation. It had been quite impossible for the small remnant of the Czech Jewish community either to redistribute or to preserve such a collection, and with Rabbi Reinhart's immediate encouragement Westminster Synagogue opened its doors to this precious remnant. The arrival of the scrolls, still wrapped in their original plastic covers and bearing their German labels, will remain in the memory of all who were present. They lay on the marble floor as if in shrouds, before being taken upstairs to be placed carefully on specially prepared racks. The huge task of examination, repair and redistribution was a unique project which has continued for nearly forty years.

As a first stage members helped to arrange and sort the scrolls so that they could be properly examined. Every scrap of parchment, paper and wrapping that might provide further information had to be carefully preserved, before professional scribes could begin work. Mr Estorick gave a lecture on the background to the project and a steady stream of visitors came to Kent House to see the moving display. The publicity given to the arrival of the scrolls inevitably brought some murmurs of disapproval as well as much encouragement to those involved. Several letters to *The Jewish Chronicle* suggested that Westminster Synagogue, as a non-orthodox congregation, was unsuitable for the work; but these doubts were outnumbered by many expressions of good wishes and offers of help. A trust was set up to handle

8. *Some of the Czech scrolls awaiting repair and redistribution*

the administration, with a Czech Memorial Scrolls committee to deal with the day-to-day running of the project; Frank Waley was the chairman and Eric Estorick was at hand as an adviser. The trust decreed unequivocally that no commercial considerations should be involved, and that when the scrolls came to be dispatched to recipient congregations, they should be held on permanent loan. This approach has always characterised the work of the trust; many requests were received to buy scrolls (some perhaps with the intention of reselling them) but the trust has always retained ownership. Should a recipient cease to make use of the scroll for any reason, it must be returned, to be reallocated to another applicant.

At about this time the synagogue received the generous gift of a set of twelve lithographs by Marc Chagall of his stained glass windows in the Hadassah Hospital synagogue in Jerusalem. They represent the twelve tribes of Israel and were executed in Rheims in 1961. In the same year Chagall created lithographs of the designs in a signed limited edition of 150 sets. The windows themselves are eleven feet by eight, and the lithographs accurately convey the message of the stained glass and the 'singing' quality of the colours. They were hung around the walls of the Reinhart Library. The first picture, on the north wall, is of Joseph, and the clockwise order then follows that of the Jerusalem windows: Reuben, Simon, Levi, Judah, Zebulun, Issachar, Dan, Gad, Asher, Naphtali and Benjamin. Most are accompanied by a text from the blessing of Jacob in the book of Genesis, and carry symbols and imagery from the biblical text. A fuller description of the designs will be found in Appendix A.

As the months passed the synagogue maintained a lively programme of activities: dinner dances, lectures, musical evenings and Purim entertainments, all of which were well supported. At the second Shavuot supper Joseph Leftwich, the guest speaker, spoke about Israel Zangwill, whose centenary year it was. When Winston Churchill died, the Sabbath morning service started earlier than usual, so that the whole congregation could watch the funeral on television.

The Czech Memorial Scrolls committee now had the invaluable services of Ruth Shaffer, who was to remain in charge of its work for many years. Ruth, the daughter of the writer Sholem Asch, with her husband Reginald, had been early members of the synagogue. They moved to Brighton after his retirement and when he died she continued to commute to Kent House several times a week to carry on with her work Her devotion to the project and her meticulous attention to a lengthy and often difficult task, cannot be too highly praised. Some years later, at nearly ninety years of age, she

9A. *Ruth Shaffer working in the Scrolls Centre*

effortlessly transferred all the trust records from their original index cards to a computer system. The committee was by now fully involved in the project, and in June 1965 a Solemn Assembly was held at Kent House to mark the completion of the preliminary work and the start of the redistribution of the scrolls. The synagogue was particularly pleased to welcome the Chief Rabbi, the Very Rev. Israel Brodie who read, in Hebrew and English, a memorial prayer for the martyred communities of Moravia and Bohemia. Some hundred guests represented the entire Jewish community, the Israeli Embassy, many non-Jewish organisations, and clergy and academics of other faiths. A message from the president of the Prague Jewish community expressed 'heartiest wishes for the dignity and full success of the memorial meeting.' A smaller reception followed a few weeks later to welcome Donald

9B. *David Brand, the sofer, repairing damaged scrolls*

Coggan, the Archbishop of York, who visited Kent House to see the scrolls and receive one of them as a gift for his diocese. Those present on this occasion included the Rev. W. W. Simpson, the Secretary of the Council of Christians and Jews. Another scroll was presented to James Parkes for the Parkes Library at Southampton University. Dr Parkes had made an important contribution to studies in anti-semitism and Jewish-Christian understanding, and he welcomed the gift warmly.

In the same year Harold Reinhart celebrated fifty years in the ministry. The congregation marked the occasion by assigning to him a mitzvah he had never before performed: he carried and elevated the scroll, to the great approval of a large number of worshippers. A reception was held after the service at which the Reinharts' old friend, the Rev. Ephraim Levine, of the New West End Synagogue, gave a witty and moving speech. The Reinharts were by now well settled in their flat on the top floor of the building. The elegant drawing room, furnished by Flora with her usual good taste, overlooked Hyde Park. She and Harold were always fond of fine antiques, paintings and embroideries, and the flat housed treasures patiently assembled over their long married life. Many friends will remember their enjoyable dinner parties, afternoon teas and receptions, watched over by the stern eye of their severe but loyal helper, Mrs Marsh.

Despite its steady growth, Westminster Synagogue, like many such organisations, was always short of money. A new method of fixing members' subscriptions, confirmed at a special general meeting, required each member's contribution to be individually agreed, rather than following a fixed scale. Some members found their subscription considerably increased, but the members' contributions committee, headed by Ivor Connick, went about its work carefully, inviting congregants who felt the sum to be beyond their means to meet them to discuss the matter.

One particular reason for ensuring that the synagogue's finances were on a sound footing was the need for an assistant minister. A small committee under the chairmanship of Leo Bernard had been trying for some time to find help for Rabbi Reinhart, and an adequate salary had to be available if their search was to succeed. Harold Reinhart, now 75 years of age, remained fit and energetic, but it was clear that the time was approaching when he would have to make way for a younger man. Several ministers and student rabbis took part in Sabbath services, and another young rabbi with his own congregation in London preached at Kent House in November of that year. Rabbi Dr Albert Friedlander was meeting his future congregation for the first time. He was then minister of Wembley and District Liberal Synagogue, and known particularly for his fine translation of Leo Baeck's *This People Israel.* Regarded by the Jewish and non-Jewish world alike as a considerable scholar, he seemed to find the congregation congenial; the feeling was reciprocated.

Ten years after its foundation, Westminster Synagogue was securely established in the Anglo-Jewish community. Many rabbis in the Reform movement had occupied its pulpit and Rabbi Reinhart often returned these visits. He was also invited to many events in other parts of the community, and was especially pleased to accept an invitation to the installation of Chief Rabbi Jakobovits at St John's Wood Synagogue. Internally, the new system of subscriptions was working well, and gradually the synagogue's finances were finding a firmer footing. However, no new minister had yet been appointed, and some slight unease was noticeable among those involved in the running of the congregation. Rabbi Reinhart, like any leader who is loved and respected by his followers, seemed reluctant to relax the reins. He still attended outside meetings, demonstrations, even marches, but he was beginning to tire easily.

In the spring of 1967 the council recommended to the members that they should formally appoint Rabbi Chaim Stern as associate minister of the synagogue. Rabbi Stern had come to England from his native New York with his wife and three sons, the youngest of whom had been born while the family was living in London from 1962 to 1965. He had first studied law at Harvard but had later been ordained as a rabbi at the Hebrew Union College. He then spent some years at the Liberal Jewish Synagogue in St John's Wood. He made an excellent impression on the congregation when he gave a sermon at Kent House, and he and his family seemed happy to remain in London. Following his appointment as assistant minister, he was warmly welcomed at a special service at which the synagogue also celebrated its tenth birthday. Speaking on that occasion, Rabbi Reinhart said that he felt that in spite of all that had been achieved in those ten years – or perhaps because of it – his task remained demanding; much was required of the congregation if they were to realise their original hope of constructing a synagogue where each member could put the gift of his spirit in the service of the sacred cause. The following month he drew attention to the fact that from that time the monthly letter to members would be from both the ministers of Westminster Synagogue. Accordingly Rabbi Stern wrote a personal message, stressing his hope that all members in his care would fulfil their obligation to play an active part in synagogue affairs, and saying that he was happy to join a synagogue where an atmosphere of devotion prevailed.

The Reinharts' Golden Wedding anniversary was also celebrated that summer and as the seasons passed the congregation continued to sponsor a regular programme of events. Rabbi Stern gave special attention to the young people's group and achieved good attendances. During the year a new friend was warmly welcomed at Kent House. It had become a matter of urgency that the Czech Scrolls Trust should find more regular help for the repair and refurbishment of the scrolls. Answering a knock at the door one morning, Ruth Shaffer was confronted by an evidently orthodox Jew, who had noticed the synagogue's name plate at the front of the house. 'Do you by any chance have any torah scrolls for repair?' he asked. 'Oh yes,' she replied, 'we have 1,564. Do come in!' David Brand came in, and stayed for more than thirty years. As an expert sofer he was doing the work his father and grandfather had done before him. His strictly orthodox beliefs were such that he would never take as much as a cup of coffee at Kent House, nor touch the hand of any woman there; but he was greatly liked and respected by all who met him and he became a very welcome part of the synagogue family.

Two of the scrolls from Czechoslovakia, once they had been carefully examined, had been set aside for the use of the synagogue itself. Flora and Harold Reinhart had together designed the covers and these were beautifully embroidered by Beryl Dean, of the Royal School of Needlework. The original designs have been preserved, and in a letter to Miss Dean Rabbi Reinhart wrote, 'The large scroll cover with a crown is inscribed in Hebrew with the words 'crown of teaching', which imply the sovereignty of divine direction in life. The second cover on which is a sprouting scroll reads 'It is a tree of life to them that lay hold of it; and they that hold fast to it are happy. Its ways are ways of pleasantness and all its paths are peace." The original tracings show flowers weaving through the letters 'W.S.' below the date in Hebrew and English. In pencil is written: 'gold copper russet brown – bit turquoise'. Rabbi Reinhart's meticulous attention to detail is shown in an attached note, 'From the line through the centre of the broad horizontal strokes of the Hebrew letters, the stitches will point at right angles to each other.'

In July 1968 family reasons prompted Rabbi Chaim Stern to return to America. He wrote to the congregation to wish members well for the future. 'I am sad that it has not proved possible for me to remain with you,' he said. Once again the search for a minister was resumed, and other matters called for attention. At the annual general meeting in November, both Sir Seymour Karminski as president, and Frank Waley as chairman of the council resigned their offices, both feeling that after eleven years they should make way for younger men. Frank was persuaded to take on the less onerous post of president, while Lewis Golden took over as chairman. His most immediate concern was to find assistance for Rabbi Reinhart. One possible candidate was a young student, Henry Sobel; it was thought possible that he might take on the post after his graduation.

Meanwhile Rabbi Reinhart's health was giving cause for anxiety. He seemed to be having some difficulty with his sight and to be in discomfort when moving about. Mrs Reinhart warded off enquiries with mention of sciatica, but those who knew him well felt that something more serious was amiss; he looked pale and thin, and was unable to attend the executive meetings in June and July. For much of the time he was confined to the flat upstairs, where a devoted and skilful nurse helped Flora to care for him. In August of 1969 he was admitted to the Middlesex Hospital and it was clear that nothing more could be done to defeat the cancer that had invaded his body. Flora spent every day and night beside him, and members of the congregation took turns to be at his bedside. Harold Reinhart died in the early morning of Sunday, 17 August. A few of his closest friends were with him, and recited the Shemah with Flora as he slipped away.

CHAPTER V

THE INTERREGNUM

On 18 August 1969, every member of the congregation received a telegram from Frank Waley: 'Our beloved Rabbi Reinhart died Sunday. Funeral Golders Green Crematorium at 11 o'clock on Tuesday. No flowers please. Congregational prayers Kent House 8.30 Tuesday evening and public memorial service Kent House, Sunday 7 September at 3 o'clock. Frank Waley, President, Westminster Synagogue.' Three days later the cremation took place, with prayers the same evening. The coffin had lain at Kent House, and as the little procession left Rutland Gardens for Hoop Lane, a courteous policeman, forewarned by Mr Bradley, held up the traffic in Knightsbridge. At Flora Reinhart's specific request the funeral service was conducted by Leo Bernard, Ivor Connick, Ezra Dingoor and Lewis Golden; Lewis later gave an address at the evening prayers at Kent House.

Harold Reinhart had expressed a wish to have his ashes scattered at the grave of Morris Joseph at Hoop Lane, and this was done in a quiet and private ceremony on 22 August. Morris Joseph, Harold Reinhart's predecessor at Upper Berkeley Street, was the author of *Judaism as Creed and Life*, a book which he greatly admired and for which he had provided an introduction to a new edition. The last monthly letter from the minister to his congregation had been sent out some four months before his death, and the chairman, Lewis Golden, had taken on this task until a new minister could be appointed. On 29 August he included in the letter the tribute he had given at the evening prayers on the day of the funeral. 'As the life of the synagogue unfolded, by his example we were to learn that selfless devotion to others brought its own reward: a full, happy, exciting life, infinitely more precious than material riches or public acclaim . . . he was never too busy, never too weary, never too sick to answer the cries of this his family, or even of the wider community . . . we mourn the passing of a great man.'

Messages of condolence from many parts of the world were sent to Mrs Reinhart, and the synagogue received generous offers of help both for the services (the High Holydays were not far ahead), and in the management of the congregation. Rabbi Sidney Brichto, of the Union of Liberal and Progressive Synagogues, was ready to put his organisation at Westminster's disposal, and a similar offer of assistance was received from the R.S.G.B. Though these suggestions were much appreciated, it was generally felt, especially by Mrs Reinhart, that a 'do-it-yourself' operation would be more appropriate. The chairman suggested that because of the singularly intimate and affectionate relations between the late Rabbi Reinhart and his congregation it would be best at present for members to carry out the duties and undertake the services that Rabbi Reinhart would have performed.

The Times carried a full obituary, describing Rabbi Reinhart as 'a man of sweet disposition, whose gentleness was combined with great practicality.' One of his former students, Jacob Petuchowski, by then a distinguished rabbi in America, who had visited and preached at Kent House on several occasions, wrote in the journal of The Central Conference of American Rabbis: 'He was averse to denominational labels, striving instead for an unqualified Judaism; and he rejected the increased emphasis on institutionalism and organisational structures in modern Jewish life'. Another old friend and colleague, Rabbi Samuel Atlas, recalled in a private letter, his 'dedication to Jewish ideals, his fervour and love for the God of Israel.' Rabbi Cassell in Bulawayo wrote of him as 'my beloved friend, cherished colleague, and revered teacher', and reprinted for his own congregation the last sermon Rabbi Reinhart had given at the West London Synagogue.

At the Memorial Service on 7 September, attended by a large number of members and by visitors from many Jewish and non-Jewish organisations, Leo Bernard said in his address. 'We speak of him as he once spoke of Morris Joseph, as 'a hero of the spirit . . . a lifelong seeker of the high and broad ideal in Judaism.' That ideal was always whole and clear in his mind and exhilarating in his heart, and he served it with a truly heroic strength and constancy of purpose.' The service was conducted by members of the congregation, and at its conclusion Mrs Reinhart, proud and composed as ever, escorted by Frank Waley, led the way downstairs, where she greeted many of those present. An equally moving little memorial service was given for the children, and Lily Cohen, who together with her twin sister Clare Diamond, was a founder member, gave a short address. 'As your teacher', she told the children, 'he encouraged you to come to synagogue, for he wanted you not only to learn about your Jewish heritage but to carry out the duties which are part of it.'

The appointment of a successor to Harold Reinhart was now crucial to the survival of Westminster Synagogue. The young student, Henry Sobel, had returned to America, and however ably and enthusiastically members carried out the various tasks of an active and vigorous congregation, they could not continue indefinitely without a spiritual leader. Amongst the possible candidates one man stood out; he had experience in leading a congregation, and having known Harold Reinhart for some years he understood the origins of the congregation. Albert Friedlander had been born in Berlin in 1927, escaping with his parents, his sister and his twin brother, to Cuba. From here his parents sent the children to foster parents in Mississippi. He graduated from the University of Chicago, reading philosophy, and attended the Hebrew Union College in Cincinnati, where he was ordained rabbi in 1952. His first rabbinical appointments were at Fort Smith, in Arkansas and at Wilkes-Barre, in Pennsylvania. On a brief visit to London he met Evelyn Phillips, and they were married at Upper Berkeley Street. They returned to America, where Albert became religious counsellor at Columbia University, where he received his PhD. Albert and Evelyn came back to London in 1966, and he served as rabbi at Wembley Liberal Synagogue until 1971. Evelyn herself was born in London, showing early musical talent

10. *The synagogue's menorah*

when at the age of eleven she played the piano at the Royal Festival Hall. She went on to graduate as LRCM at the Royal College of Music.

The ministerial committee, under the chairmanship of Leo Bernard, were unanimous in their decision to invite Albert Friedlander to come to Kent House as often as he could, on a regular basis if possible, on the understanding that he would leave Wembley as soon as his contract could be amicably terminated; the synagogue would be guided by lay leaders until a permanent appointment could be made. Rabbi Friedlander generously agreed in any event to give temporary help. He preached in the synagogue once a month, held a weekly study group and assisted frequently when a rabbi's help was needed. The congregation also had the benefit in these difficult days of a young temporary minister, Alan Mann, a student rabbi and acting minister of the Woodford and District Liberal Jewish Synagogue. He undertook to reorganise the young people's group under the name of the Southwestsevens, and helped out with services and with many of the tasks then being undertaken by members.

The question of a memorial to Harold Reinhart was discussed by the council in February 1970, and a committee was appointed consisting of Leo Bernard, Doris Herschorn and Kitty Stein; it was asked in particular to consider the possibility of publishing a memorial volume of some kind. The expansion of the Reinhart Library was also suggested.

At the 12th annual general meeting, the chairman introduced a new form of annual report and printed accounts, prefaced that year, and every year since, by the congregation's Statement of Principles and Policy. He thanked all those members who had helped to achieve the continuity of synagogue services, so important to the life of the congregation, at a time when it had no religious leader. He mentioned also the debt of gratitude owed to the organist Harold Lester, who now felt that a new instrument was much needed for the synagogue, and hoped that by the next High Holyday services Kent House would have 'the finest electronic organ that money could buy'. The chairman then moved on to the most important item on the agenda, a recommendation to members to approve the appointment as minister of Rabbi Dr Albert H. Friedlander. It was explained that although Rabbi Friedlander could not undertake to come to Kent House until 1972, he might be released a year earlier, if his Wembley synagogue found a successor. The meeting accepted unanimously the proposal that Rabbi Friedlander be appointed.

The Harold Reinhart Memorial Fund was opened in July, inviting contributions from members towards a number of commemorative projects. A Harold Reinhart Memorial Lecture was set up in association with the Society for Jewish Study, of which Rabbi Reinhart had been a prominent member. The first lecture, entitled 'Religion and Social Welfare' was given by Sir Seymour Karminski, and the series continued for twenty-five years. In collaboration with the Leo Baeck College a Reinhart studentship was established; the first beneficiary was Stephen Katz, the son of Rabbi Reinhart's old friend and colleague, Rabbi Arthur Katz.

The synagogue library, which had benefited greatly from the help of Norma Waxenberg, was developing well. Some excellent shelving had been designed and donated by Mr Joshua Manches, a good friend of the congregation, and installed by Mr Jones, a cabinet-maker who had done much fine work at Kent House. A facsimile edition of the Golden Haggadah, of which the original fourteenth century manuscript was in the British Museum, had been donated by a generous member. It was placed in a glass cabinet set into the shelves and care was taken to turn over the pages from time to time. A tablet of green-veined marble was put up on the north wall of the library, a gift from Rabbi Reinhart's old friends, J. Samuel & Sons. It read:

THE REINHART LIBRARY
HAROLD REINHART
First Minister of Westminster Synagogue
1957–1969

The new organ was installed just in time for the High Holyday services that year. The makers were Copeman Hart, and as the parts were carried in Mr Hart and his helpers began the intricate task of assembling them. The console was designed by the architect of the first floor work at Kent House, Thomas Pan, and the loudspeakers were inserted into the west wall by Yeoman and Partners. This work was carried out over several weeks, all signs of the installation being cleared away before every Friday night service. In his note to the congregation about the new organ, the gift of generous members, the chairman wrote: 'When complete the organ will contain almost a thousand separate oscillating electrical circuits, using transistors, to give the sound of a large traditional pipe organ, for each circuit is equivalent to a pipe. It will use four treble loudspeakers and two bass loudspeakers to give a comparable range. In situ the organ will be 'voiced' just as one would 'voice' a pipe organ; voicing is the process of adjusting the quality of each note to suit the building.' An inaugural recital on the new organ was given by Harold Lester, during which he explained the musical construction of the instrument, and demonstrated its wide range, in a programme which included works by Handel, Bach and Cesar Franck.

By the beginning of 1971 work had begun on the construction of a flat for the Friedlander family on the second floor at Kent House. Rabbi Friedlander had come to an agreement with the Wembley synagogue to release him so that he could take up his appointment with Westminster earlier than had been expected. Meanwhile Lewis Golden's two years as chairman of the council came to an end. When Harold Reinhart died Lewis had realised the need for an executive chairman who could take on some of the work normally handled by the rabbi. He rose to the occasion admirably, spending much of his time at Kent House and sparing no effort to ensure that all went well. His professional acumen and the meticulous way in which he undertook every task stood the congregation in good stead at a difficult time. Lewis himself had been unwell and felt he should hand over his onerous responsibilities to someone who could undertake an 'active, vigorous, executive leadership'. He had been a warden at Upper Berkeley Street and had held office at Westminster Synagogue since its inception. He was a chartered accountant, having qualified after the war. During his military service he reached the rank of Major in airborne forces, the 'red berets', and had taken part in the battle of Arnhem. Later he wrote an important book, *Echoes from Arnhem*, describing the role of the signals units as well as his own experiences; he remained in close touch with his regiment. He was later to play a leading part in the administration of the London Library, serving as treasurer and then as chairman, for which achievement he was awarded the OBE. His wife Jacqueline came from an old Sephardi family. Her grandmother, Estrea Aelion, known to many Westminster members, lived to the age of one hundred and four, and was recognised in her later years as an authority on the Ladino language; she recorded a programme of Ladino songs when well into her nineties.

The office of chairman was now taken by Albert Polack, though it was understood that he could serve for only a limited time as he and his wife were due to retire to Clifton later that year.

By July the congregation was able to look forward to the induction service for Rabbi Friedlander. His flat was nearly ready and a kiddush was arranged as an opportunity to meet not only the new rabbi, but also his wife Evelyn and his daughters, Ariel and Michal. The congregation was particularly glad to welcome on that occasion Rabbi and Mrs Stanley Dreyfus of New York. Mrs Dreyfus was the grand-daughter of Dr Leo Baeck, who greatly influenced Rabbi Friedlander and the progressive community as a whole. This family occasion was followed two weeks later by a formal induction ceremony, and Westminster Synagogue found itself with a new rabbi.

CHAPTER VI

THE FRIEDLANDERS

In 1971, the year that the Friedlanders came to Westminster, Leo Bernard took the place of Albert Polack as chairman of the council. Leo had been active in many aspects of synagogue life, and was warden elect at West London at the time of the secession; but he too resigned when Harold Reinhart departed. At Westminster his readiness to address the congregation on Sabbath mornings made him a useful 'stand-in' for the ministers, but he resolutely insisted that these were 'talks' rather than 'sermons'.

By the time of the High Holydays the Friedlander family were beginning to settle down at Kent House. It can hardly have been easy, especially for the two small girls, to find in a formal town house the freedom and relaxation they had enjoyed on the outskirts of London. However, members were delighted to have young people living in the house and the family were soon happily involved in the life of the congregation. Albert Friedlander was much occupied with both Jewish and inter-faith affairs. He was chairman of the Conference of European Progressive Rabbis, and in 1972 welcomed its members to Kent House for their annual meeting. The synagogue apparently gave the guests such an excellent lunch that in spite of the claims of the French, Dutch, German and Swiss delegates, it was considered that London was the best venue, gastronomically speaking at least, for their discussions. Rabbi Friedlander was also playing an important part in the affairs of the Leo Baeck College, and several of its student rabbis preached at Westminster Synagogue. He was assiduous in continuing, and enlarging, the congregational activities that had been established in earlier years. The guest of honour at the Shavuot Supper was Martin Gilbert, who spoke on 'Churchill and the Jews'. A second discussion group was set up to study the Jewish philosophers, and the Southwestsevens youth group flourished. Not only did its members take part in sponsored walks, enjoy debates and discussions, and participate in social service activities; they were also cajoled into painting the children's classrooms with the active help of their rabbi.

At the annual general meeting the chairman suggested that three characteristics had shaped the synagogue's identity: seriousness of effort, care and discrimination in the synagogue, and independence of spirit. Rabbi Friedlander expressed his pleasure at the prospect of building on those foundations. Two particularly happy events followed in 1972. One of these occasions was the celebration of the synagogue's first twin confirmation, the bar-mitzvah of David Connick and the bat-mitzvah of his sister Lesley. Their parents, Ivor and Claire, were founder members of the synagogue, and the twins had been brought up as regular and enthusiastic participants in Sabbath morning services. Many of their friends recalled two tiny voices piping up 'Amen' a fraction after the rest of the congregation, when the twins were too small to see the Ark from where they sat. They read their portions on that day with the skill typical of their family tradition. To commemorate the occasion the congregation was presented with a silver breastplate, designed by Rabbi Reinhart, for the synagogue's smallest scroll. A silver scroll marker was also presented on this occasion. The congregation had always refrained from identifying such welcome gifts by a prominent acknowledgement, and none of its fine possessions bear, in any obtrusive way, the name of the donor.

Ivor Connick had always played an important part in Westminster Synagogue affairs. Although from an orthodox Ashkenazi background (he had been brought up at Ealing United Synagogue) his regular participation in Westminster's services brought a fluent Sephardi accent to his familiarity with the prayer book. Over the years he has remained one of the most eloquent readers at Sabbath and Holyday services. His legal training at the London School of Economics proved invaluable when he was called upon to serve on the council and executive of the congregation. Claire had grown up at Upper Berkeley Street, where she had attended religion classes and had joined the junior membership. Her life-long habit of referring to the

11. *Rabbi Albert Friedlander* OBE, *minister to the congregation from 1971 to 1997*

Reinharts as 'Uncle Harold and Aunt Flora' marked an affection that was warmly reciprocated. Both the Connicks played a leading part for many years in the work of ORT.

The synagogue also welcomed in 1972 the opportunity to present a gift to Albert and Betty Polack on the occasion of their golden wedding, and of Albert's eightieth birthday. As founder members and greatly valued participants in the affairs of the congregation, they were presented with a dinner service as an expression of the great affection and regard in which they were held by their fellow members.

Not since the birth of the children of the Noble family in the early years of the twentieth century had a child been born at Kent House. The congregation was therefore particularly happy to welcome the arrival of Noam Friedlander on 8 October 1973. Her mother, Evelyn, left the synagogue at the end of Yom Kippur (the day of the outbreak of the Yom Kippur War) to go straight to St George's Hospital, where Noam appeared the following morning. Whether it was because her parents' flat was on the second floor of Kent House, or because she was an especially well-behaved child, Noam never made herself heard during the synagogue services, nor did she disturb any other events at Kent House. She was later blessed in the synagogue by her father's old friend and colleague, Rabbi Hugo Gryn.

Twenty years after its inauguration, the congregation had inevitably lost a number of its founder members. Bob Toeman, Sam Ansell, Leonard Stein and Krissie Vale had died, and the loss of Sir Seymour Karminski, the first president, was particularly keenly felt. His distinguished legal career – he was a Lord Justice of Appeal and Privy Counsellor – did not prevent him from serving the Anglo-Jewish community. He was president of the Jewish Welfare Board and gave his help to many other causes. His wife Susan was also involved in Jewish affairs and remained active in the synagogue after his death. Not long afterwards another founder member, Doris Herschorn, died. Her quiet modesty and her loyalty to the Reinharts and to the synagogue were memorable, as was her generosity on many occasions. At the funeral service Rabbi Friedlander spoke of her as 'a woman of worth, whose upright character, fine intellect and generosity of spirit, would be remembered as a blessing.' Her son, Hugh Sassoon, has continued to play an important part in synagogue affairs.

During the 1970s London was a centre of an IRA bombing campaign. Several explosions were audible from the synagogue and its proximity to the barracks made it vulnerable. A device detonated outside Harrods caused considerable devastation and was heard clearly during the Sabbath service. The presence of the Turkish Embassy at the bottom of Rutland Gardens required a police officer to be permanently on duty there, a reassuring presence at a time of considerable tension. Later the Iranian Embassy siege, a few hundreds yards further west, brought home to the congregation an awareness that London's peace and security were always fragile.

Rabbi Friedlander's participation in Jewish and non-Jewish activity in the wider community continued to grow. He spoke frequently on the radio and appeared on television, representing the progressive movement in discussion programmes and inter-faith debates. He had close links with his more orthodox colleagues, and the congregation was especially pleased to welcome the Chief Rabbi, the Very Rev. Immanuel Jakobovits to Kent House to give a lecture on 'Jews and Medicine', a subject on which he was a foremost authority. He explained the traditional Jewish approach to medical ethics, mentioning in particular the sanctity of human life in relation to birth control, abortion, transplant surgery and euthanasia. Those present were aware of the significance of the Chief Rabbi's visit to Kent House, where he was later welcomed on a private visit to the Czech Scrolls. It may be that his readiness to visit Westminster Synagogue was influenced by the congregation's independence; it had never formally joined any progressive group. In 1957 *The Jewish Chronicle* had noted in a headline 'New London Congregation to join Association of Synagogues', but although the matter had been discussed from time to time, the council had never considered such a move to be appropriate; it has always been felt that an independent synagogue had a useful part to play in the closely organised Jewish community. However, many Reform and Liberal rabbis were welcomed at Kent

House to preach and to take services. Rabbi Friedlander on his part visited many Progressive synagogues. He was now Director of Studies at the Leo Baeck College (later to be made Dean) and served on the governing body of the World Union of Progressive Judaism. It should be mentioned that the West London Synagogue and the Reform Synagogues of Great Britain (formerly the Association of Synagogues in Great Britain) continued to be helpful to Westminster Synagogue in such matters as burial rights and access to the R.S.G.B.'s rabbinical court.

For some time the Reform synagogues had been planning a new Daily and Sabbath prayer book under the editorship of Rabbi Lionel Blue and Rabbi Dr Jonathan Magonet. Dr Magonet visited Westminster Synagogue to explain something of the problems they had encountered in preparing a text which would be faithful to tradition and yet in harmony with contemporary idiom. After some consideration, however, the council decided that the needs of the congregation would best be met by the earlier version, until such time as an entirely new prayer book could be prepared by the synagogue itself.

On the twentieth anniversary of the founding of Westminster Synagogue, a special appeal was launched with the aim of raising the capital sum necessary to discharge the mortgage on Kent House; this fell due for redemption at the end of the year. The synagogue's finances were now on a firmer footing, though members' subscriptions did not adequately cover all outgoings. The activities committee was still hard at work with fund-raising projects to meet the shortfall. One regular fund-raising event was Evelyn Friedlander's admirably organised Bring And Buy Sale at Kent House. Over the years these sales brought in very useful contributions to the synagogue's funds.

Now under the guidance of Constance Stuart, the first woman to take the chair, the synagogue turned again to a subject which had concerned its members since its inception: the age at which bar-mitzvah should be celebrated. Twenty years earlier Harold Reinhart had written to the congregation on the occasion of the first bar-mitzvah to be celebrated in the new synagogue to explain his reasons for preferring confirmation at fifteen or sixteen years of age instead of the traditional thirteen. He had emphasised the form the ceremony should take: the young person was to read the lesson from the scroll, with the translation and the blessings, together with a prayer. Boys and girls were to be treated in exactly the same way, and the words 'confirmation' and 'bar-mitzvah' were used synonymously. The only disagreement concerned the age at which the ceremony was to take place.

Rabbi Reinhart had been particularly anxious that whatever age was chosen – and he preferred sixteen, believing thirteen to be too young for the formal acceptance of such religious responsibility – it should be the same for all. 'I have never been able to understand congregational usage,' he wrote, 'that will have thirteen for those who wish it, sixteen for those who want that, and both for those who like both. This is the way of weakness, trying to be all things to all men. As a pedagogue and as a minister, I could not be a party to such an anarchic procedure.' He went on to explain the changes that had occurred since mishnaic times, when a girl of thirteen could be married and a boy was held fully responsible for his actions. In deference to his views a majority of the congregation agreed to adopt sixteen as the standard age for bar- and bat-mitzvah.

In spite of the unease of some parents, most of the young people in the congregation were confirmed in their sixteenth year, which allowed for the ceremony to take place before the strain of school examinations. In 1979, however, some members raised the matter again, suggesting that there should be a choice of age for their children's confirmation. The council felt that this was too important a matter to resolve without first obtaining the views of the membership as a whole; and each member was sent a copy of Rabbi Reinhart's original memorandum together with a letter from Rabbi Friedlander, who agreed in the main with his views. Rabbi Friedlander mentioned in particular the importance to the synagogue's religion school of pupils who continued their studies beyond the age of thirteen; they were able to take 'O' level Hebrew if they wished, and at the later age they were able to participate in synagogue services. 'Our ritual,' he added, 'as we have it now is the envy of many congregations who have found that their own ceremonies have become just family observances of a merely routine kind.'

With these two papers, members received another letter, from Dr Michael Sinclair, a council member, who would have liked parents to have a choice of the age at which the ceremony should take place. He felt that it should be 'as early in adolescence as possible, thus creating a foundation of religious belief and social responsibility.' The congregation was asked to communicate their feelings in the matter to the council, which judged that 'no significant number of members desired any change', and agreed to continue with the existing policy.

During the ten years since the death of Rabbi Reinhart, several projects had been proposed as a memorial to him, and the Reinhart Library, established on the occasion of his seventieth birthday, was growing steadily. A particularly welcome accession was arranged by Ralph Yablon, who had acquired a large collection of books from the library of the former Chief Rabbi, Dr Israel Brodie. Many of these books were donated to the Reinhart Library with the ready approval of Dr Brodie. One project, however, needed particular care. By the beginning of 1981, the synagogue was proud to publish *Harold Reinhart, 1891–1969, A Memorial Volume.* The book was compiled by Lewis and Jacqueline Golden, with a memoir of Rabbi Reinhart by Leo Bernard. It comprised a selection of Harold Reinhart's articles, notes and letters, giving a vivid account of his qualities as man and minister. In a review in *The Jewish Chronicle*, Chaim Raphael said that the book brought out 'his sense of urgency and involvement, dominated always by his feeling that in every situation a Jew had to frame his appropriate response to it in spiritual terms.' The book was handsomely printed and produced, and copies are still available.

The summer of 1982 was of particular significance to members of Westminster Synagogue. Twenty-five years had passed since the momentous meeting at the Royal Empire Society which brought the congregation into being. The president, Lewis Golden, recalled the birth of the synagogue in his address at the annual general meeting. He spoke of the 'wandering Jews' with their portable Ark, though there had been 'nothing ad-hoc, nothing make-do, nothing amateur about the arrangements.' Sadly, a short time before the anniversary celebrations, Albert Polack died at the age of ninety-one. No member of Westminster Synagogue had exerted a greater influence on the congregation, not least in his scholarly but unpretentious addresses on many Sabbath mornings.

The principal event of the twenty-fifth anniversary celebrations was a service of thanksgiving at Kent House on Sunday, 25 July. Some two hundred members and their friends came to the service. The special guests included the Lord Mayor and Lady Mayoress of Westminster with their chaplain and his wife, Rabbi and Mrs Hugo Gryn from the West London Synagogue, the principal of the Leo Baeck College, the chairmen of both the Liberal and Reform synagogue associations and many other communal representatives. Harold Lester and Ronald Spector presented, together with Esther Salaman, music much of which had been composed especially for the occasion.

Several of the synagogue's founder members, including Rabbi Cassell, participated in the service, and the special prayers included some composed by Rabbi Reinhart. In his address, Lewis Golden spoke of the congregation's regard for the City of Westminster, where it had always worshipped. He recalled the devotion and hard work of the members who had served first alongside Rabbi Reinhart, then alone, and finally with Rabbi Friedlander. 'We need our synagogue,' he said, 'we need its strength; we need its inspiration; we need its comfort; we need its fellowship; we need its enlightenment; we need its encouragement'. Lady Karminski, who was unwell, sent a message in which she recalled visits to dances at Kent House as a young girl 'in pretty dresses, dangling programmes . . . men in tails, white ties and gloves.' She had helped Flora Reinhart to bind the supports of the Chuppah, and with many other tasks that needed attention at Kent House. She welcomed the coming of the Friedlanders, and mentioned in particular Evelyn and her daughters, Ariel, Michal and Noam. 'I have always found,' she added, 'that the greatest strength in any organisation lies in a happy family unit at the head.'

Rabbi Friedlander in his closing prayer gave thanks for the many blessings that had been granted to him as its rabbi for more than a decade, 'surrounded by loyal friends and by high ideals and faith which would surely be realised in the years to come.' After the service tea was served in the Rutland room. The whole house was decorated with flowers and the doors to the newly created roof garden were left open for visitors to see one more aspect of the gracious building where Westminster Synagogue had its home.

It is surely true that the progress of a community is reflected in the lives of its members. David Golden, the little boy who kindled the Ner Tamid at the first service at Kent House, brought his own daughter to be blessed before the same Holy Ark some twenty-five years later. At about the same time the congregation bade farewell to one who had greatly influenced its endeavours since the beginning. Flora Ruman Reinhart was a memorable figure both in character and in appearance. Her tiny person, silver hair immaculate, accompanied her beloved Harold wherever his ideals took him. Always seated in the same place in the synagogue, she never missed a service. She was no mere shadow of her commanding husband, however. Her high standards put many in awe of her, but the quiet help she gave to those less fortunate than herself was long remembered. Her ashes, like those of Harold Reinhart, were scattered at Morris Joseph's grave.

Three years later the congregation celebrated another silver anniversary, as it completed twenty-five years at Kent House. The member who was largely responsible for the purchase of the house died that year. Ralph Yablon, a solicitor from Bradford and prominent in business life, had also been instrumental, with others, in arranging for the Czech Scrolls to be brought to the synagogue from Prague, and had always played an important part in the running of Westminster Synagogue. He was president for six years and his generosity and encouragement was always much appreciated by members.

The Czech Memorial Scrolls Trust had continued for some twenty years to restore the scrolls and distribute them on loan to Jewish congregations and other applicants all over the world. Many visitors came to Kent House to see the scrolls and never failed to be deeply moved by the experience. The trust had always looked forward to creating a permanent record of its work, for inevitably the number of scrolls still available would come to an end. Indeed the number of those that were 'kasher' – suitable for use in services – was already much reduced and the trust was aware of the importance of preserving their history. Since Flora Reinhart's death the flat on the third floor of Kent House had lain empty. The remaining scrolls were housed on racks outside the flat, next to the room where the scribe worked and where the packing could be done. A small committee had been set up by the synagogue to determine the best use of the remaining rooms on the third floor. It was felt inappropriate for the flat to be let commercially, as access would have to be through the synagogue premises. An agreement was accordingly drawn up by the synagogue for the top floor to be leased to the trust to enable it to build a centre displaying the story of the scrolls. The trustees received a visit from the project director of the Smithsonian Institute in Washington. She was shown the scrolls and with a colleague spent some time discussing the possibility of organising a scrolls museum at Kent House. On her return to America the officers of the Smithsonian sent a detailed plan to the trustees for discussion. Their proposals involved some structural work on the top floor of Kent House and a great many changes to the way in which the Scrolls were presented. The cost of the operation, including professional fees, would have been in the region of £75,000, and the trustees felt that such an elaborate presentation would be inappropriate for the simple message they wished to convey. Tempting as the outline proposals were, it was agreed that in the tradition of Westminster Synagogue, a 'do-it-yourself' operation would be preferable. Philippa Bernard undertook to set up the centre as a small museum, and this was achieved for less than one tenth of the cost of the original plan. Nevertheless, it made use of showcases and display screens of excellent quality, together with suitable lighting and furnishings and carefully prepared information cards. The first room was employed as a reception area, with office facilities, comfortable chairs and a television set to enable a video of the scrolls project – made by an American company – to be shown. The two rooms overlooking Knightsbridge were used as the exhibition halls, depicting the arrival of the scrolls in London, the restoration work of the scribe, and

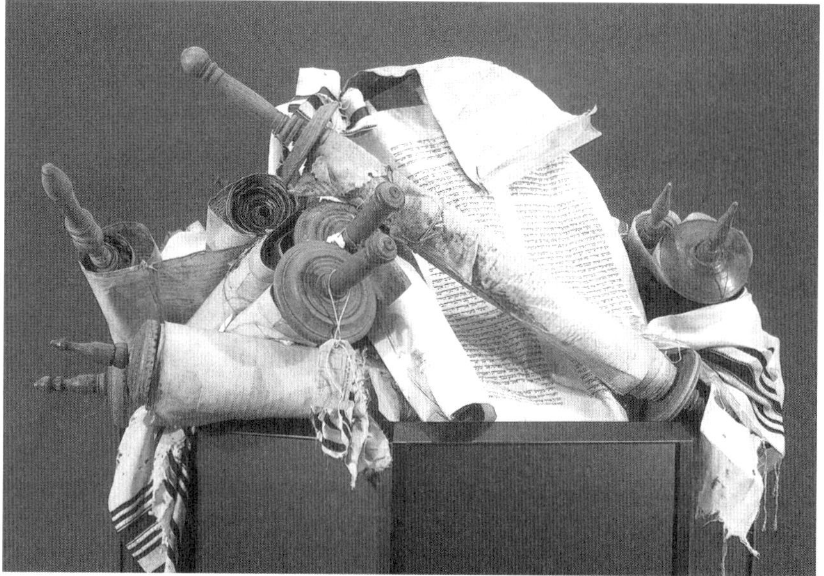

12. *The display of damaged scrolls and tallitim at the Memorial Scrolls Centre*

accounts of the reception of the scrolls in some of their new homes. A large map showed how the scrolls had been distributed and another indicated the towns of Moravia and Bohemia from which they had come. A few were displayed in the showcases, and the central feature of the main room was a moving exhibit of damaged scrolls, swathed in tallitim, and conveying silently the tragedy of the Czech communities overwhelmed by the Holocaust.

With the help of the Textile Conservation Service at Hampton Court Palace, a number of binders which had been wrapped around the scrolls when they arrived were impressively displayed in a wall showcase. This collection of binders is believed to be among the largest in the world. The corridor from the reception area to the main rooms displayed a collection of Torah illustrations in the form of early engravings, lithographs and postcards.

The formal opening of the Centre took place on the morning of Sunday, 3 July 1988 in the presence of the Lord Mayor of Westminster, councillor

Elizabeth Flach, Mr Hroneck, chargé d'affaires at the Czech Embassy and several other guests. Honorary officers of the synagogue were present and Rabbi Friedlander returned from study leave in Germany for the occasion. The president, Lewis Golden, in his speech of welcome, recalled those who had made the centre possible: Rabbi Harold Reinhart, Eric Estorick, Ralph Yablon and in particular Frank Waley, the first chairman of the scrolls committee, who had died at the age of ninety-four a few months previously. Rabbi Friedlander read a message from the Chief Rabbi, Lord Jakobovits, who described the collection of scrolls as 'a tribute to the wonderful dedication of all involved'. He also mentioned that the sacred objects of the Prague Museum had been assembled, under the direction of the Nazis, by his late uncle Tobias Jakobovits, who had worked there as librarian and was later deported with his wife to Auschwitz, where they died. 'I look at the centre,' he said, 'as a living monument to their memory.'

Thereafter the scrolls centre was open twice a week, and many visitors, both adults and children, came to see the display and the scrolls still awaiting restoration; a booklet telling the story of the project was available. The committee continued to receive requests for scrolls, but by this time none remained which answered the strict requirements for synagogue use. Many were sent out, however, as memorials – to the White House, to Windsor Castle, to the London Library and to York Minister among other recipients – and members of the committee frequently visited synagogues, schools and other institutions to speak about the project.

Anyone who owns a house will understand only too well that there is no limit to the work – and money – needed to keep it in good order. So it was with Westminster Synagogue; the maintenance work needed at Kent House to keep it running efficiently and to avoid major expenditure at a later time, made heavy demands on synagogue funds, as did the creation of the scrolls centre on the third floor. By the mid-eighties it had become necessary to rewire the whole house, to overhaul the central heating and ventilation, to remove a dangerous chimney, to attend to the lift, which had become disturbingly inefficient, and to deal with a seemingly endless succession of problems. The response to a serious attempt to raise the necessary finance by means of a building fund was inadequate, but a series of fund-raising events were successful socially and went some way towards filling the widening gap between income and expenditure. Nevertheless, the future of the congregation seemed uncertain. Not only were its financial affairs giving cause for concern, but attendances at services and at synagogue activities were discouraging. Something of the momentum of the early years had inevitably been lost, and it was becoming increasingly difficult to find members willing to take on the various tasks essential for the smooth running of the congregation. The appointment of wardens was a particular problem, due perhaps to the fact that Westminster Synagogue, like Upper Berkeley Street, was a metropolitan rather than a neighbourhood congregation. Parking regulations, children's school commitments, the demands of business life, all added to the difficulties. The chairman at that time, Christopher Rees, speaking of these problems, refuted the idea that the small group of members who ran the synagogue would not welcome new volunteers. He invited members to contact him with offers of help of any kind, but the response was disappointing.

The council, too, was disturbed. At a meeting called to plan for the future an unusually large number of council members were present. They discussed the poor attendances, the failure of some members to pay their subscriptions promptly and the severe financial problems facing the synagogue. Urgent repairs and restoration of the building were costing far more than the congregation seemed able to afford. At the annual general meeting which followed, the president, Lewis Golden, told members that a number of those attending the earlier council meeting had promised to help, and invited the members to follow their example. Already there had been rumours about the sale of the building, and these were quickly dismissed by the president, though he did concede the possibility of some form of redevelopment.

The apparently insuperable difficulty of financing a major rebuilding programme led to the formation of a Kent House development committee, which met at the end of 1989 with the synagogue's architect, Thomas Pan. Its remit was to evaluate a plan drawn up by Norman Winbourne, a surveyor and member of the synagogue, to develop the southern wing of the building. This would enable that section to be sold for commercial purposes, bringing the congregation a substantial income and allowing it to retain the main part of the house for its own use. Several alternatives were suggested, all of which involved surrendering a large part of the building.

Plans were also drawn up for car parking in the front garden, for meeting safety requirements and for seeking the necessary local authority permissions. The budget seemed to indicate that the cost of development would be about £450,000 and sale receipts about £1,350,000, giving a surplus of some £900,000. In all communications with local residents and planning officials, the committee was at pains to emphasise that the purpose of the development was not to indulge in the speculative construction of office accommodation for profit, but to raise sufficient funds for the refurbishment of the whole building, together with a properly organised maintenance schedule. The plans were submitted to Rutland Court, South Lodge and Rutland House (to the south of Kent House). The preferred plan involved two additional floors above the ground floor of the south wing, with a new lift and air conditioning, and in April 1990 the synagogue council was invited to approve a confidential report explaining the development. It was made clear to council members that an office development was considered preferable to a residential one for financial reasons, but that inevitably some loss of amenities would follow. A caretaker's flat would be constructed in the basement, but the room used by the youth group would be lost. The kitchen would be relocated in the existing vestry area and the first floor library would be surrendered to the new building, as would the roof garden. The minister's flat was to remain as it was, and on the top floor the room where the Czech scrolls were housed would also be used as the workshop. The financial consequences of these far-reaching redevelopment plans were explained to the council and they were asked to comment on the project. The plans were duly approved and the development committee was asked to submit a planning application to Westminster City council.

Some opposition to the project was put forward by the Knightsbridge Association, whose chairman, as it happened, was a member of Westminster Synagogue. The objection was to office accommodation in a residential area, but when it was realised that Rutland Gardens already contained several commercial premises, the chairman's attitude changed. Westminster City council, too, had reservations about the scheme for offices. Their objection seemed to be that although they accepted that the synagogue constituted a special case, they might be setting a precedent which would in time alter the environment of Rutland Gardens. However, another problem had an even greater influence on the proposed development of Kent House. This was the collapse of the property market, closely linked with an economic recession. The synagogue report of 1991/92 told members: 'Work on endeavouring to find a profitable proposal for developing the SW corner piece of our land has now been suspended, due to the poor state of the property market. It is impossible to contemplate any speculative venture for the time being. Having established that planning consent for a commercial development is most unlikely, a residential scheme was investigated. There might be a variety of possible solutions which could be worked up when prospects improve.'

When Westminster Synagogue came into being, the congregation made use of the prayer books used by the West London Synagogue. Some years later, revised editions were produced by the R.S.G.B. and Westminster considered carefully whether these should be adopted. However, the style of the new version was not unanimously liked, and it was decided that the existing book should remain in use for the time being. By 1990 there were insufficient copies and many were worn and shabby; the prayer for the royal family was obsolete and it was said that some members of the congregation were still praying for Queen Alexandra! Some other passages were out of line with modern thought. A prayer book committee was set up, and decided that the best way forward was to reprint the existing book with some revision of its structure and vocabulary. Professor David Raphael agreed to head a liturgy committee to proceed with the project. Some of the problems it encountered needed a mandate from the council. Was the use of such terms as 'mankind' and 'forefathers' sexist? Did 'thou' and 'thy' rather than 'you' and 'yours' sound archaic? One member of the council insisted that if his wife fell into the ocean he would shout 'man overboard'! All such minor difficulties were duly overcome, and the *Daily and Sabbath Prayer Book* was published in the summer of 1992. Two versions were printed, one in cloth, and the other bound in leather with a silk marker.

The new prayer book was inaugurated at a Sabbath morning service, followed by a congregational kiddush. In his preface Professor Raphael wrote, 'Ever since its foundation in 1957, Westminster Synagogue has used the *Daily and Sabbath Prayer Book* (sixth edition) of the West London Synagogue of British Jews and its allied congregations, now known as the Reform Synagogues of Great Britain. In 1977 the R.S.G.B. replaced that prayer book with a radically revised seventh edition. Westminster Synagogue retains close associations with the R.S.G.B. and joins in many of its activities. On the liturgy, however, most members of Westminster Synagogue feel a strong attachment to the prayer books to which they are accustomed. Being now faced with the need to reprint or replace the *Daily and Sabbath Prayer Book*, the council has decided to retain the main substance of the old book with some limited change. A few prayers and readings have been added, the number of psalms in the later part of the book has been reduced, and the English translation of Hebrew prayers and texts has been revised.

'We wish to express our warm gratitude to the West London Synagogue for allowing us to make use of the text of its former prayer book and for relinquishing to us any copyright that may still obtain; and likewise to the Oxford University Press, who hold the copyright in the Hebrew setting of the sixth edition, for allowing us to reproduce it.' The congregation felt deeply indebted to Professor Raphael for his scholarly work.

CHAPTER VII

A NEW LEADER

Rabbi Friedlander had taken up his post as minister of Westminster Synagogue in 1971 and would reach his seventieth birthday in 1997. He had undergone serious heart surgery and though he had made a good recovery he had inevitably become less active. His work outside Kent House continued to take up a good part of his time, and his wife, Evelyn, apart from her radio broadcasts, was much involved in the discovery and presentation of Genizah material – the stores of books and other material in Europe hidden from the Nazis and rediscovered many years later; she had set up the Hidden Legacy Foundation to handle the work. The Friedlanders' daughters were grown up and following their own careers, and it seemed appropriate in these circumstances for Rabbi Friedlander to consider retirement when a successor could be found; it was envisaged that this would be in the summer of 1997, leaving some two years for the necessary arrangements to be made.

The appointment of a new rabbi was bound to be a challenging task. The synagogue had been in existence for less than forty years and had been founded under unique circumstances. The Reform community in the UK had grown steadily but it was likely that most potential candidates were already known to the congregation. After consultation with the R.S.G.B. the following note was circulated:

'Westminster Synagogue is seeking a rabbi who will replace Dr Albert Friedlander on his retirement within the next 2–2½ years after 26 years distinguished service. Westminster Synagogue is an independent community but has close links with the Reform movement, using its own and the West London prayer books, as well as the services of the R.S.G.B. Beth Din. The synagogue has a membership of 506. It is envisaged that the successful candidate will be paid according to the salary scale recommended by the R.S.G.B. In addition, a flat at Kent House will be available.

The rabbi is expected to perform all the usual functions of a single handed rabbi in a Reform community including acting as principal of the religion school which is held on Sunday and has a roll of 30 children.'

By the end of the year one particular candidate had been proposed for the position, though for personal reasons he was unable to commit himself until the following year, and it was in any case necessary for any offer of the post to be confirmed by the members in general meeting. In the spring of 1996 the congregation was informed that Rabbi Charles Middleburgh was to be appointed as the new minister of Westminster Synagogue. A press release was issued and at the annual general meeting the president, Ivor Connick, said 'We have been truly fortunate in our two religious leaders over the past thirty-nine years. Both the late Harold Reinhart and Albert Friedlander have been an inspiration to us and have attracted a devoted following. I have no doubt that Charles Middleburgh will prove to be a worthy successor.' But this was not to be. Rabbi Middleburgh was offered the position of executive director of the Union of Liberal and Progressive Synagogues, and decided to give this offer precedence. As the committee resumed its work Rabbi Friedlander, who was to become minister emeritus when his successor was found, was on sabbatical leave at the university of Frankfurt. His place at Kent House was taken temporarily by an old American friend, Rabbi Ezra Spicehandler, who with his wife Shirley was always a welcome visitor to Westminster Synagogue.

The difficulties of finding a new leader were not eased by the simultaneous efforts of the development committee to find a suitable method of utilising part of Kent House in order to obtain much needed income. The demands on the congregation's finances were pressing. A major overhaul of the organ had been completed and some essential refurbishment of the house was carried out, even though much of the work depended upon the redevelopment plans.

On November 9 that year the congregation welcomed as guest preacher

Rabbi Thomas Salamon. In his sermon Rabbi Salamon noted that the day fell on the anniversary of the Kristallnacht massacre, and spoke movingly of its reverberations in the contemporary world. He was warmly welcomed at a kiddush after the service by the president and by the chairman, Edward Glover. He visited the synagogue again during the following April and in an amusing note in the newsletter of that month Rabbi Friedlander reminded his readers that when a new pope was to be elected, the word 'papabile' appeared next to a likely candidate's name. Such was his feeling about Rabbi Salamon that he claimed to have seen white smoke rising from the organ that morning, and the congregation knew that it had a new leader!

Rabbi Salamon's appointment was duly confirmed by the members in general meeting, and all were delighted to welcome him, with his wife Renée, his son Aaron, and his mother Alice into the congregation. Rabbi Salamon was born in Kosice in 1948 and came to England twenty years later. He studied for the rabbinate first at Jews' College and then at the Leo Baeck College where he was ordained in 1972, the youngest rabbi ever to be ordained there. He served at the West London Synagogue for three years, then went to Norwood where he became executive director. In 1980 he studied law while serving as a part-time rabbi at the Hertsmere Progressive Synagogue. He then decided to become a full-time rabbi and was appointed to his present post at Westminster Synagogue.

Rabbi Friedlander's departure from office was much regretted. Although he was to serve as rabbi emeritus, and the Friedlanders were to retain their flat on the second floor of Kent House, the congregation had had the benefit of his leadership for some twenty-six years and would miss him greatly. Members were able to express their good wishes at a dinner at which 260 guests attended. Colleagues and friends joined in the celebration and their feelings were summed up by Rabbi Louis Jacobs: 'Long may you continue to be a powerful force for Anglo-Jews and world Jewry.' The Friedlanders were presented with two volumes of messages of goodwill, poems, photographs and children's drawings, together with a cheque from well-wishers to enable them to realise their life's ambition to travel around the world.

13. *Rabbi Thomas Salamon, minister of the congregation from 1997*

Rabbi Salamon took up his post on 1st September 1997. He wrote to the congregation in the newsletter: 'A synagogue should not only be a place of worship but also an educational meeting place, a centre for people to gather, meeting whenever at all possible the needs of the community . . . I believe that a synagogue, our synagogue, should be just such a place, where we try to answer questions; the place which provides the tools and the means if required, where all are welcome and take part, where all are encouraged to be active, be it just for a minute or a little longer.' Sadly, Rabbi Salamon's first sabbath service coincided with the funeral of Diana, Princess of Wales, and for only the second time in the synagogue's history the time of the service was changed. It began at 5.30 pm and concluded with a special prayer and memorial service, followed for the first time by a Havdalah service.

The synagogue held an induction service for Rabbi Salamon on 1 February. The guests included the Lord Mayor and Lady Mayoress of Westminster, and Peter Brooke, the City's Member of Parliament. The service was led by Rabbi Charles Emanuel, with a special prayer by Rabbi Curtis Cassell. Ivor Connick welcomed the Salamon family to Kent House and Rabbi Friedlander formally inducted Thomas Salamon and pronounced the priestly blessing. Westminster Synagogue's new rabbi told his congregation that he looked forward to a constructive and rewarding future with his new community, and thanked them for his warm welcome. The music for the service was arranged and played by Harold Lester, together with his daughters Gaby on the violin, and Vicky on the harp; Mark and Julia Glanville led the singing. At a reception after the service many of the members present had an opportunity to greet the Salamons.

Members of the congregation were well aware that negotiations were taking place over the development of Kent House; however, they had not as yet been informed of what the development committee had in mind, and no detailed plans had been revealed. Vincent Wang, a member of the congregation and a property developer, had taken over the chairmanship of the committee, which included Ivor Connick, Edward Glover, Hugh Sassoon, Constance Stuart and Jack Zunz. It was by now quite clear that any development had to be of a residential nature, but the committee was faced with a number of options. It seemed that if the synagogue was to preserve its own facilities while developing the southern end of the building, the construction of one large house rather than several flats might best serve the purpose. Vincent Wang told the committee that he had been advised that lofty spaces carried a premium, and plans could be made for an 'upside down' house, with grand public rooms at high level, enjoying the splendid views and light. The targeted buyer would be a special purchaser for whom 'normal property arithmetic' would not be a factor. Architects suggested various schemes, ranging from the demolition of Kent House altogether, and replacing it with an apartment block, to converting the front of the present building into luxury flats, with an entirely new synagogue at the rear. The synagogue council, presented with these somewhat drastic possibilities, decided first to find out the cost of putting the house into good order and securing its future. If the amount raised from the proposed development were to prove inadequate there would be no point in proceeding.

Needless to say the prospect of demolishing Kent House met with firm resistance, and the committee was informed that planning permission would in any event be more favourably considered if the old house were retained with its present frontage on Knightsbridge. Accordingly the synagogue sought and obtained planning consent for a new residential development on the rear one-third of the site, keeping the front two-thirds for the congregation's own use. This area was then examined to find ways of increasing the number of seats in the synagogue which had a clear line of sight to the Ark and the reading desk, of improving the facilities of the Czech Memorial Scrolls Centre, and of extending the accommodation available for festivals, classrooms, offices and other synagogue activities.

Once the formalities concerning planning permission for the development were complete, members of the congregation were fully informed about the plans. It was envisaged that either a block of five apartments or a single house of roughly the same size would be built at the rear of the site. However, this would entail relinquishing in the basement the classrooms, lavatories and boiler room; on the ground floor, the vestry, kitchen and caretaker's flat, together with one third of the Rutland room; on the first floor, the whole of the far end of the sanctuary, the small library and the flat roof; on the second floor part of the Friedlanders' flat; and on the third floor the Czech scrolls rooms as well as the fire escape. The wholesale surrender of such a large part of the synagogue premises was felt to be too great a sacrifice, and the development committee decided to renegotiate the planning permission and reduce the area of the site available for rebuilding. Some members felt that the sanctuary itself should be redesigned, either by moving the Ark into the north-west corner or by some means of improving the participation of members hidden from the Ark and reading desk during the festival services; but others disliked the idea of any such radical alterations to the room. Other considerations for the refurbishment of the house were to be improved offices for the rabbi and staff, better classrooms for the children, modernisation of the kitchen, better accommodation for the Czech scrolls and a more efficient fire escape. It was also felt that if suitable space could be made available for hire purposes this might provide a useful source of additional income.

While these possibilities were under discussion, Rabbi Salamon was much occupied with his special interest in the care and education of the children of the congregation. His wife Renée had been awarded the Advanced Diploma in Jewish Education at London University's Institute of Education, and she had agreed to undertake the improvement and restructuring of the religion classes at Kent House. In the early months of his ministry Thomas had examined closely the best way of bringing children (and their parents) into more active participation in synagogue life. It was decided that because of the increasing commitments – social and educational – of young people, classes would be held on Saturdays instead of Sundays, and this quickly increased the number and enthusiasm of those attending. It had been hoped that while their children were under instruction in the basement classrooms, parents would attend the service in the synagogue. This part of the plan proved to be a little optimistic, but the interest shown by the parents in the new arrangements was encouraging.

Other measures to bring the children into the heart of congregational affairs included family services, the introduction of the children attending the classes into the last part of sabbath services with a special kiddush, and an invitation to children who had already celebrated their bar- or bat-mitzvah to take an active part in those services. The enthusiasm of the children was increased by a number of visits and other extra-curricular activities. They visited the Czech Scrolls Centre upstairs at Kent House, a Chagall exhibition, and also Hammerson House, the Jewish retirement home, where they helped to take the Sabbath service. A special children's Seder and a Purim workshop were introduced which enabled the students to take an active part in the preparations for the festivals. The religion classes were renamed Or Shabbat (Light of the Sabbath).

As well as the establishment of Or Shabbat, other changes were quietly taking place in the running of the congregation. The long-standing problem of finding three members willing to take on the onerous position of warden was solved by the drawing up of a list of volunteers who were prepared to serve in this capacity from time to time. The senior warden was then able to arrange a rota of colleagues who were not committed to constant attendance, but were all experienced in acting occasionally as lay leaders. By this time the wardens' morning suit and top hat had been abandoned in favour of less formal attire and yarmulkas, and for the women wardens – there had so far been three: Cynthia Landes, Sylvia Raphael and Ann Fischer – suitable every-day clothes. This was a change that had often been debated by the council, with some more conservative members reluctant to abandon old-established custom – but broader minds prevailed. A regular kiddush after the Sabbath morning service enabled congregants to meet each other informally.

The prayer book committee was reconvened, once again under the chairmanship of Professor David Raphael, to produce a new Festival Prayer Book. The excellent *Daily and Sabbath Prayer Book*, which they had published previously, encouraged the congregation to ask Professor Raphael and his committee to repeat their achievement.

A much-valued member of staff retired in October 1998. Rosemary Henriques had served as secretary to the congregation for twenty-two years, knowing almost all of the congregation by name and giving invaluable help to rabbis and members alike. In addition to administrative abilities, Rosemary was a skilled and creative florist, and the synagogue was frequently filled with beautiful floral displays for which she was responsible. The congregation owed her a great deal and wished her much happiness in her retirement.

In October of 1998 the congregation was sad to learn of the death of Rabbi Curtis Cassell. He had been a founder member of Westminster Synagogue when he and Rabbi Reinhart departed from the West London Synagogue. Although he then moved to Bulawayo to serve as minister to the Reform congregation there, he always kept in close touch with events at Kent House, and visited the synagogue whenever he was in London. When he returned to London for good after his retirement he often took part in the services, giving sermons and helping out whenever he was needed. In 1996, on the occasion of his diamond wedding and the sixtieth anniversary of his ordination, he wrote a pen portrait of himself, recalling some of the memorable features of his life, and mentioning in particular the loving, loyal and active support of his wife Ceci. At a memorial service held at the Liberal Jewish Synagogue in St John's Wood, Westminster Synagogue's Peter Goldsmith, who had known the Cassell family well in Bulawayo, recalled Rabbi Cassell's achievements there. He had been able to co-operate successfully with his orthodox and Christian neighbours, as well as with black members of the local community. Leo Bernard, too, spoke on that occasion of Rabbi Cassell, describing his sermons as wholly unpretentious, quietly eloquent and extraordinarily wide-ranging. A large congregation from across the Jewish community and beyond remembered him affectionately and felt a great sense of loss. Westminster Synagogue was privileged to receive from Rabbi Cassell's family a substantial part of his important library.

After the retirement of the synagogue's caretaker, Patrick Cummins, who with his wife Christine, had served admirably for a number of years, the congregation was faced with some difficulty. The flat at the far end of the ground floor was urgently needed for additional classrooms. The synagogue religion classes had expanded steadily, and this important synagogue activity had a prior claim on such rooms as were available. It was therefore decided for the first time to dispense with a resident caretaker and to find a suitable replacement who would work on a daily basis. The choice was a most fortunate one. Daniel Daren (known to all, then and now, as Danny) became a member of the 'family' from the outset. Jewish in part himself, he had seen military service in North Africa and then joined his family firm in the textile business. Never known to lose his temper or pull a long face, Danny became an invaluable asset; working long hours, at ease with members, visitors and staff alike, he became an indispensable, much-loved part of the community.

At the end of the century the world was somewhat nervously awaiting the new millenium. Sufficient time has now elapsed to recall with amusement the almost medieval attitudes that some imaginative sects adopted. Concerns about health services, finance and other areas vulnerable to computer breakdown were more rational, but all these anxieties proved ill-founded. Jews had, by and large, kept their feet on the ground, but even their leaders were prompted to give voice to forecasts of the future. Rabbi Salamon's predictions anticipated the replacement of the Chief Rabbinate by a democratic council of rabbis, electing its own leader, which would seek co-operation with the rest of the Anglo-Jewish community; the reassessment of their role by the progressive elements of that community, with a period of harsh questioning and turmoil; Israel's efforts to assert its authority, with a huge debate ensuing with the diaspora; and a great redistribution of power in world politics. 'I believe that we are entering an exciting period,' he said, 'and we must be vigilant'. These predictions were not perhaps as doom-laden as those of the Hebrew prophets, but they were at least partly fulfilled. What he did not envisage, or perhaps preferred not to reveal, was an enormous upheaval closer to home.

CHAPTER VIII

REFURBISHMENT AND RENEWAL

The difficulties of the development committee in obtaining the necessary planning permissions and embarking on a complex expansion programme for Kent House seemed almost insuperable. Plans for two schemes for the development of the synagogue itself were presented to the congregation, but members were divided in their views on the new ideas, anxious about the inevitable disruption of services and of other activities, and apprehensive about the alterations to the sanctuary. Financing the new building would be an expensive venture and would clearly involve a very long-term investment. At the council meeting held on 29th April 1999 Lewis Golden put forward the idea of raising from within the community itself whatever was needed in order to retain the whole of Kent House and to refurbish it completely; he promised to give the project his family's support. The idea was accepted and members were approached accordingly, many proving extremely generous.

It was thought that about £1,000,000 would be needed, but even that huge sum eventually turned out to be insufficient. The Memorial Scrolls Trust agreed to provide a large donation, in place of the annual rental it had been paying to the synagogue. During the year fund-raising efforts added to the total, and timely new Inland Revenue regulations that year enabled tax exemption to be claimed for even small charitable gifts. Early in 2001 the new chairman, Howard Leigh, was able to congratulate the congregation on achieving its financial goal, anticipating that the work could begin towards the end of that year.

In the spring Rabbi Salamon was admitted to hospital for a serious operation. His place was taken for a while by Rabbi Friedlander with the help of members of the congregation; but happily the annual general meeting was able to welcome him back, with a warning that he must take life a little more easily! This injunction could not easily be obeyed, for the contractors were due to start work, and Renée Salamon was at the forefront of the refurbishment committee. However, by juggling her commitments, with several balls in the air at once, Renée managed to make the necessary arrangements for the work to begin.

It seemed at first that it might be necessary for the congregation to move out of the house while the builders were at work. Various temporary locations were considered, among them the German church in Kensington and an abandoned synagogue in Notting Hill; but it was felt by all concerned that however uncomfortable it might be, the congregation should 'camp out' at Kent House.

When the surveyors, architects and builders examined the house more closely, it became clear that the fabric was in a worse state than anyone had imagined. Parts of the exterior stonework were crumbling, the roof leaked, and the lift was considered unsafe. The refurbishment committee accordingly gave priority to essential aims – making the building weatherproof and safe, providing new classrooms and enabling the premises to be made sufficiently comfortable and efficient to attract additional income in the future. Tenders were invited for the work and a professional project manager appointed to oversee the operation.

Meanwhile the congregation was doing its best to maintain 'business as usual', and it was delighted to congratulate its rabbi emeritus on being awarded the OBE for his inter-faith work. Apart from Westminster Synagogue's own appreciation of his achievements, Rabbi Friedlander was warmly congratulated by leading members of non-Jewish organisations. Sister Margaret Shepherd, NDS, director of the Council of Christians and Jews, wrote a charming recollection of him: 'I remember marvelling at his ability to head a workshop at the annual Jewish-Christian-Muslim conference in Bendorf with his usual expertise and wisdom, whilst keeping a very young daughter, Nomi, happy as she played on his lap.' A few months later a further honour was bestowed upon Rabbi Friedlander when he became the first rabbi of a non-orthodox congregation to be made a president of the Council of Christians and Jews.

Or Shabbat went from strength to strength with a new and enthusiastic teaching staff and a wide-ranging programme for the growing number of students. Even before refurbishment commenced, a local nursery school expressed interest in renting space in the basement as soon as the rooms were ready.

In the spring of 2002 the appearance of Kent House brought home to members, and indeed to passers-by, the magnitude of the refurbishment project. Scaffolding and plastic sheeting enveloped the whole building, carpets and floors were covered, doors screened off. Hitherto unknown stairs and passages appeared, dust lay everywhere. The extent of the work had inevitably grown, with new plumbing, wiring and mechanical needs. The two top floors were vacated, the Scrolls Centre temporarily closed, and the Friedlanders moved to a flat nearby. The tender documents from the builders, available for members to see, were some five inches thick, and the administration of the synagogue suffered endless difficulties with telephones and computers. Each stage of the work seemed to bring to light additional unpleasant surprises, but one aspect helped those who were caught up in the upheaval: almost without exception the workforce was amiable and considerate, with a sense of humour and a genuine curiosity as to what went on in the place it was refurbishing.

The principal goal was to have the sanctuary ready for the High Holydays. Meanwhile services were held in the Rutland room, as in the congregation's earliest days at Kent House. A quiet and intimate atmosphere prevailed there, with the small portable Ark from Caxton Hall days brought into use once again. The race against time to get the main sanctuary ready involved overtime and weekend work, but it was done. The curtains, now nearly forty years old, were cleaned and re-hung. New carpeting had been generously donated, and the new lighting and sound systems were in place. Although the heating arrangements were behind schedule, the Holydays fell early that year and the weather was kind. The decorations in the synagogue and in the rest of the house followed as nearly as possible the original colours and styles. Kent House was not a listed building so no stringent regulations covered the refurbishment work; however, application for a lottery grant from English Heritage was under consideration, and therefore any changes to the structure and decoration needed to conform to the original appearance.

The considerable amount of additional work that had proved necessary involved the committee in some far-reaching decisions. The sum available for immediate use covered only what was needed to put the building into acceptable condition. In consequence the first phase was confined to essential work on the exterior, the opening up and renovating of the basement, new wiring, heating and communication systems, redecoration of the administrative offices and the sanctuary, and necessary improvements to the lift. If further finance were to become available, possibly with a grant, then the congregation would be able to undertake work on the second and third floors, put in another entrance at the rear, with a stair tower to the top of the building, and enjoy such 'luxuries' as new chairs, curtains and furnishings wherever needed.

The formidable amount of planning, costing, supervision and decision-taking were under the control of the refurbishment committee. Two members of that committee, Renée Salamon and Ann Fischer, undertook the day-to-day control of the work. They coped heroically with many difficulties, and without their devoted attention the successful completion of Phase I could never have been achieved.

This brief account of the first stage of the refurbishment of Kent House – a greatly encouraging though somewhat traumatic event – seems an appropriate point at which to conclude the story of nearly half a century of synagogue life. Those who played a part in the early years can take some pride in what has been achieved; those who have come more recently to the congregation will surely be aware of that achievement and build upon it.

The synagogue will of course be playing its part in a community greatly different in many respects from that in which it started its life, and no-one can predict the issues and the influences which will shape Anglo-Jewry in the coming decades. Nevertheless, the continued independence of Westminster Synagogue in a closely organised community will surely remain a valuable asset, and the synagogue's Statement of Principles and Policy will continue to guide its future.

REMINISCENCES AND RECOLLECTIONS

Many members have enhanced this book with their memories of synagogue life. The few that follow come from a cross-section of the congregation.

CYNTHIA LANDES *and her husband Leonard first attended Westminster Synagogue in 1962 after seeing an announcement in* The Jewish Chronicle *for High Holyday services, but they were slow to make up their minds and did not become members until 1968. Leonard, who died in 1994, became junior warden in the year that Harold Reinhart died, and was still a warden when Albert Friedlander became the minister. Cynthia became a warden in 1984, the first woman to do so. Their daughter, Anna-Rose Jackson is also a member, although she now lives in Birmingham with her husband and two young sons.*

Mr Bradley, our first resident caretaker, had to go into hospital. Leonard, then senior warden, and I, in charge of hospitality, were summoned to Kent House, to be shown how to operate the huge safe in the kitchen. I still have a note of the manoeuvres needed to open and close the heavy door – so many half and quarter turns of the lever to the right or left. The door was always too heavy for me to manage, and I don't remember whether Leonard ever succeeded in following the instructions, but I still have them. Scrawled on an envelope and tucked into my hospitality notebook for 1970 and 1971, they are part of synagogue history. There, I noted that six dozen crusty rolls were ordered from Harrods, four (old) pence each, to be delivered on the morning of Tuesday, 9th June, for the Shavuot supper; that the small tea urn held thirty-five cups and the tall urn forty-two cups (according to the notes you could get twenty-four cups of coffee from a jar of Gold Blend Nescafe, cost six shillings).

Some time in 1971, before Albert Friedlander was able to take up the position of rabbi to the congregation, the main part of the second floor was being decorated as a flat for the Friedlander family. It must have been at the time when Mr Bradley was in hospital, since Mrs Reinhart was alone in her flat at Kent House on the third floor. She was not afraid to be alone in the building, but accepted a subterfuge, which probably deceived no-one, so that the builders working on the second floor would not realise that she was on her own every night. So every morning at 7.45 Leonard was let into Kent House by Flora Reinhart. When the builders arrived at 8 he was there to open the door as if he lived there, and five minutes later he left for work. This charade continued for some time, probably until Mr Bradley returned to work.

DAVID RAPHAEL *came from an orthodox community but joined the Reform movement first at Maidenhead and later at Westminster. During a brilliant academic career at Oxford, in Otago, New Zealand, at Glasgow and finally at Imperial College, London, he published several books, the most recent being* Concepts of Justice. *The loss of his wife Sylvia affected him deeply and many members will recall the eulogy he gave for her at Kent House at that time. He was a warden of the synagogue, as was his wife – the second woman to hold the office. Professor Raphael was at one time chairman of the council and continues to play an important part in synagogue life.*

My wife and I joined Westminster Synagogue in 1973 when we came to live in London. Why Westminster? Both of us had been brought up as orthodox Jews but in synagogues of a tolerant spirit. Garnethill Synagogue in Glasgow, which we attended during our twenty years there, was a firm supporter of Dr Louis Jacobs in the controversy about him, and seriously contemplated a formal association with his congregation. The excellent children's choir at Garnethill was made up of boys and girls alike, including our two daughters, whose attachment to Judaism owes quite a lot to that. We therefore were put off by the segregationist attitude of the United Synagogue when we moved to England, and preferred to join a Reform synagogue. When we visited Westminster we were impressed by the minister, Rabbi Friedlander, and by the executive member who dealt with newcomers, Ivor Connick.

We have been thoroughly happy at Westminster. When the council decided to open the office of warden to women, my wife was glad to serve as the second woman in that capacity (Cynthia Landes was the first) for a full three-year term, ending up as senior warden. At the same time I was chairman of the council. I had declined an earlier invitation to act as warden because I thought it was antiquated to require male wardens to wear top hats and morning coats. When this practice was dropped, I felt obliged to offer my services and have acted as a warden for quite some years now.

I think that the major contribution of my wife to the synagogue was her service as warden, and consequently her membership of the council as senior warden. She was very knowledgeable in matters of Judaism and Jewish practice, and was forthright in her expression of her views. My own major contribution has been in the compilation of revised prayer books. I was convenor of the committee that revised first the *Daily and Sabbath Prayer Book*, and then the *Festival Prayer Book*. The selection of passages for addition or exclusion, and the revision of the English translation, were mainly undertaken by myself, but I should add that in translating the *Daily and Sabbath Book* I was greatly assisted by my wife, who had considerable expertise in translation and was more knowledgeable than I in Hebrew grammar. She was, alas, no longer alive when I was concerned with the *Festival Prayer Book*. She died on the night of Simchat Torah in 1996. When I attend the services of the High Holydays, I am poignantly reminded that the service of Yom Kippur in 1996 was the last at which she was present.

Both our daughters were married in Westminster Synagogue, and therefore they, too, cherish their memory of it. Rabbi Friedlander was especially helpful in guidance to one of our sons-in-law. The regard of my wife and myself for Westminster Synagogue is bound up with our appreciation of Rabbi Friedlander's kindness.

HUGH SASSOON *was born in London to a 'Berkeley Street' family. In wartime he was shipped to Canada, returning in 1943 at the age of fourteen as a passenger on an aircraft carrier. Following National Service and university, he became a Chartered Accountant, banker and investment manager. He was also treasurer and chairman of a housing charity.*

In the mid-1940s (I was a teenager) I became aware of the very close relationship of my mother (who became Doris Herschorn) and the Reinharts – evidenced amongst other things by phone calls – both frequent and long – and over the years we saw a great deal of them. I was therefore well aware of the increasing tumult at the West London Synagogue which culminated in two special meetings at Friend's House with capacity, so it seemed, greater than that provided for High Holyday services including the inevitable overflows. This in itself tells something of the feelings generated.

Our revulsion in the way matters were handled (perhaps in reaction to Harold Reinhart being no angel when roused) and our desire to part from his enemies, led naturally to our joining in the foundation of his new congregation. That the break happened was brought home by the holding of High Holyday services in 1957 at Rudolph Steiner Hall, even before the formal founding of the new congregation.

My mother became immersed in the preparatory arrangements and was an initial member of the council. I was one of the first trustees – a position I held for some thirty-four years – and as such was asked to comment on sites being examined, particularly the Church of the Holy Shepherd in Lower Sloane Street, and later Kent House.

The first fund raising was an evening at the Kensington Palace Hotel when at the end of the proceedings I made a bid for the tombola left-overs. The pedal car which had attracted me was to be much enjoyed by a growing family, but what I had not appreciated was the volume of way out gramophone records and shirts and pyjamas of extreme sizes and equally extreme colours which came with it!

It was about this time that Ralph Yablon devised a plan to warehouse shares in a hitherto family company which was being reshaped to go public. In parallel with others, I guaranteed a bank loan, the resulting overall profit of the scheme going a long way to cover the cost of Kent House. At about 9 pm, on two occasions, I found Harold Reinhart at my door, and knowing he never took no for an answer I was fearful he would sit out the night if necessary. The first request was for funds to pay for the Everlasting Light he had just bought; the second was for half of the cost of the first organ. No doubt he did this to others also.

The new synagogue was made by, and has prospered through, the tireless efforts of Harold Reinhart and many others, then and since. However, there was certainly one fundamental problem, not tackled in time: the attitude to teaching in the early days of the religion school; it is good to know that this aspect of synagogue life has now greatly changed.

EZRA DINGOOR *was born in Bombay of Iraqi parents. He came to England in 1953 and became a mechanical engineer. After National Service he joined the British Coal Utilisation Research Association and later the Central Electricity Generating Board, representing the UK on the International Electricity Council. He became a J.P. in 1984 and is a Trustee of Age Concern, Barnet. He married Eileen at Kent House in 1961 and they have two children.*

My earliest memory was of attending services at Caxton Hall; I distinctly remember the little Ark being brought into the small room for prayers. Then we moved to the exciting phase of acquiring Kent House. I had never seen so much dust and dirt, and it was marvellous to witness the dignity of labour. No task was too cumbersome. Everyone was willing to apply rust remover on to fireplaces and to clean the marble. It was patently obvious that Mrs Reinhart had done nothing like it in her life, but that did not prevent her from tackling the job with gusto! My wife Eileen and I were the first to be married in Kent House in October, 1960.

When I was appointed as warden for the first time, I recall that Peter

Blom refused to become warden unless I joined him, apparently due to his lack of confidence in reading Hebrew, and I have served as warden under all three ministers at Kent House.

I recall Frank Waley as very down to earth. When called upon for a donation he would say, 'One has to balance one's needs. As to what one is able to contribute: well, after spending on food, clothes and the odd hat for the wife, whatever is left as spare can go to the synagogue.' My memories of Harold Reinhart are very clear: if you missed attending service on the Sabbath, you were sure to be rebuked with, 'Have you found a better place to spend your Saturday morning than in the house of God?' And I often said to myself during his sermons, 'But how did he know that I had been thinking about that very subject?' Talking this over once with Jack Blacker, we came to the conclusion that Rabbi Reinhart had an uncanny knack of using such terminology that you felt that he had entered your thoughts and was addressing you personally! To watch Harold taking Flora across the road was a wonderful sight – he used to usher her across as if she was a delicate doll. It was very clear how dear she was to him – and he to her.

I have always felt at home at Westminster Synagogue, despite the fact that there are numerous synagogues within easy walking distance of my house. I am proud to say that I have participated in every High Holyday service since we moved into Kent House, and have always felt spiritually uplifted by the Kippur service. I hope that we will always have lay readers and that all our seats will remain available to any member or guest.

VALERY REES *gave up all thoughts of a career when the first of her five children came along, but she was somehow inveigled into teaching and translating Latin. She has been drawn deeply into Renaissance history, philosophy, religion, art and music and is at present working on the letters of the Renaissance philosopher Marsilio Ficino.*

I first came to Kent House at Rosh Hashanah in 1961, just a few days after our move back to London from what my mother always regarded as seven years' exile in the north. Older members will recall Krissie Vale, who had been an old friend of my mother's – they had worked together at the Board of Deputies back in the 1930s – and it was at Krissie's insistence that we now came to sample this new synagogue that was so different from those my parents had known.

For me, for some reason, it felt like coming home. Though we had sporadically attended various shuls, and I had been sent from time to time to cheders for a term or two, I had never felt I belonged to any synagogue or Jewish community beyond that of family, large though that was in those far off days when weddings could easily include three hundred guests of close relations alone! But now in Kent House I vividly recall some sort of direct connection with the millenia of tradition, and a great, guiding force. Rabbi Reinhart was surely not many steps removed from Sinai – or at least he knew how to bring that presence close.

That first year I dared to come back when the High Holydays were over. By bus and train, on my own, I attended my first Succot ever – and never really looked back. I suppose the warmth of welcome surprised me. Before I had always had to shrink from the accusing charge of 'Your parents aren't members here!' But Westminster was not like that. It clearly offered another way, whose warmth, wisdom and sheer kindness were not lost on a fourteen-year-old girl.

I suppose that is why distance and difficulty have never really interfered with my sense of loyalty and commitment, though they sometimes get in the way of frequent attendance. I can look back nostalgically now to those early years: the embryonic youth group, the philosophical tutorials on Louis Jacobs' book *We Have Reason to Believe*; making tea in vast brown pots in the dark cavernous kitchen on cold winter Sunday afternoons; the excitement at the arrival of the Czech scrolls; Rabbi Reinhart's sciatica; the first time I was asked to read in Hebrew – who could possibly say 'no' to him? A wealth of detailed memories from a world now gone.

Skip then to 1970, when Albert Friedlander's arrival meant our wedding could be celebrated in the house I so loved, as he brought his Wembley congregant, my then fiancé Christopher, with him. Then there were the years of small Reeses getting under everyone's feet and on some people's nerves, as we tested to extremes that the Westminster welcome was extended to all ages. Ours was, I believe the first wedding that Albert celebrated at Kent House. Our daughter Clare's to Yuval Keren – was by a happy coincidence the last before he retired.

And now again a new era in synagogue life, only this time I suppose we must count among the 'elders'. But that original flavour of spiritual strength and great vibrancy that made itself felt in 1961, has survived all the outward changes that the years have brought to Kent House; I am as proud to share the prospect of the next four decades as I am to look back on those past.

ALEXANDER GOLDSMITH, *16, is in the midst of his AS levels at St Benedict's school, Ealing. He enjoys reading, playing the piano, and is a member of the Air Cadets; he assists with teaching the six to seven year old group at Kent House on Saturday mornings.*

From a very early age, I can remember sitting with my father in our familiar seats (which have at times been usurped, always to be zealously reclaimed). At first, going to the synagogue meant that I would sit, slightly fidgety, waiting for the sermon, and the subsequent Kiddush, and of course, challah. However, some things intrigued me; I would sit forward in my chair for my favourite songs, and crane my neck to see the scrolls pass, and their elevation. My father would discuss the portion with me in the afternoon (if my concentration held for long enough!) and so a pleasant routine was built into Saturdays.

Gradually, I learnt more about Judaism, and about why we were at the synagogue. I started to engage with the community, with the services, and with the ideas that I came across. The synagogue is still something that is reassuringly constant in my life, as the exams flash by or loom ahead, as work mounts up or is, at a slower rate, completed. I know that I shall find in the synagogue people who know me, who will always greet me, and a place that will be both theirs and mine for some time to come. As I become more and more a member of the community, I feel a sense of satisfaction that through my (attempts at) teaching, I am welcoming others into the same environment that I have learned to feel at home in. Teaching has strengthened me (physically as well as mentally), and through it I hope and believe that both my pupils and I have benefited.

EDWARD GLOVER *is married to Juliet; they have two children, Leo and Samantha, three dogs and six cats. He is a career property financier and investor and is a director and head of property for HSBC Specialist Investments Ltd. He is interested in cricket, which he refuses to give up, and has been involved in the Maccabi movement including stints as chairman of Maccabi Association and vice-chairman of Maccabi Great Britain.*

My mother was brought up in a largely non-observant household. In deference to my father, president of the Bournemouth Hebrew Congregation (though he always said that this was because the members thought they were voting for his father!) she had been married under orthodox auspices; but she had never been really comfortable in an orthodox environment or with the idea of bringing up her son in it. As a precocious eight-year-old, I had also been distinctly unimpressed by my first experiences of an orthodox congregation, so the invitation from a neighbour to try out a new Reform synagogue within walking distance, presided over by Rabbi Reinhart, of whom my mother had passing knowledge, was timely and eagerly taken up. Westminster Synagogue had only recently been established in its intended permanent home, but both community and building made immediate and lasting impressions.

The services were a revelation. They were short and understandable, with both Hebrew and English read clearly and with expression. They were conducted with a precision of which Sir Malcolm Sargeant would have been proud, but the decorum and attention which this encouraged from the congregation enhanced their spirituality rather than detracted from it. The sermons had passion, associated in my memory with the tendency of Rabbi Reinhart's tallit to slip from one shoulder, and learning. The fundamentals of Judaism were always central, but were held with a comfort that permitted rather than excluded an appreciation of the culture and beliefs of others. A schoolboy starting out on the classics could not fail to be enthralled by the ease and total lack of pretension with which Albert Polack, recently retired from the care of the Jewish house at Clifton, would move between and compare Greek, Latin, Hebrew and English.

Being still in the early 1960s there was a certain formality. The wardens set the tone with their morning suits and on the high holidays it certainly seemed that bowler hats outnumbered yarmulkas. A tie was essential even for a schoolboy and school blazer and cap were favoured dress. The teachers in religion school were addressed with their appropriate title, never by their first name. However, the formality came from respect not stiffness or a lack of warmth.

The building was a perfect complement. The proportions of the main rooms and the sanctuary were elegant, but those of a house and home, a rather grand one, perhaps, but a home nevertheless. The secondary rooms, used for religion classes, were smaller and darker but created a sense of mystery with much to be discovered. Others have said that entering the sanctuary for a service is like going into the drawing room of an old friend, and those sentiments I share. For a religion that has a strong emphasis on home observance and has seen its ministers as teachers, not priests, the domestic scale, with the rabbi at the heart of the congregation, not elevated on some grand chair or bimah or pulpit, has always felt right. In other circumstances, the plainness of the decorations might have created a feeling of austerity, but for me at Kent House it allowed the quality of the building to show through without distraction.

The contentment of the marriage of community and building is clear. For me, as I am sure for others, it contributes much to the synagogue and its place in my life. I seldom fail to be uplifted when entering Kent House and participating in synagogue life. I will always be grateful for that introduction of forty years ago.

DAVID ADLER *is a retired chartered civil engineer, married, with two children and three grandchildren. He is particularly interested in photography and the origins of religion and spends much time with his wife at their house in France. He is the editor of* The Metric Handbook of Architectural Design Data.

My wife and I joined Westminster Synagogue about 1967 after meeting Rabbi Reinhart. After our daughter Rachel was born in 1971 she used to spend the services sleeping in her pram in the Marble Hall, benevolently looked after by Mr Bradley, the 'more-than-caretaker' to the synagogue. Mr Bradley made himself responsible for keeping the house in good condition, and turned his hand to all sorts of repairs. Over the age of seventy, he was once found sixty feet up in a large tree in the front garden, pruning it! Whenever there was a do in the synagogue, Mr Bradley would proudly produce the two highly polished samovars to dispense tea and coffee.

In those days parking around the synagogue was easy. Usually you could park in Rutland Gardens, or if not, in the park. If all else failed, parking meters were still cheap, even if you had to walk a little distance to find a vacant spot. What a change we have seen over the years.

A few years after joining I was asked to become a warden. At that time wardens wore formal morning dress with a black top hat. I acquired a second-hand suit from Moss Bros., but they could not find me a hat to fit my head. For many years I borrowed hats from Jack Blacker and from Leonard Landes – both of whom seemed to have the same shape of head!

THE RABBI RECOLLECTS . . .

It was a warm summer's day in 1996 when Rabbi Albert Friedlander and I had lunch in a small restaurant on Old Brompton Road. During that very pleasant lunch I mentioned to him that I would like to return to more full-time rabbinic work and at the same time I asked him if he had any suggestions. He looked at me and said that he was retiring and that there was going to be vacancy at Westminster Synagogue. I must admit that at that time I knew very little about Westminster, so I said that I would think about this. I started my research, and my first ports of call were several of my colleagues from both of the rabbinic movements: the Rabbinic Conference and the Assembly of Rabbis, Liberal and Reform groups respectively. I asked them what they knew about the community and without exception they told me that if I were to take the position I would get a beautiful flat in Knightsbridge and virtually rest on my laurels, as there would be very little to do: a dwindling independent community, elderly people, and so forth.

It was in September 1997, over a year from the moment of my lunch with Albert, when I took up my position at the synagogue. Indeed, it was on 16 April, 1997, my son's birthday, that the congregation decided to appoint me to succeed Rabbi Friedlander and become the community's third minister in its forty years history.

My first service was scheduled to be on Saturday, 6 September 1997, the day of the funeral of Diana, Princess of Wales, who died tragically in a car accident in Paris on 31 August of that year. So here was my first crisis: Knightsbridge was on the route of the funeral cortege and all surrounding streets were closed, so how were we going to hold our morning service? I phoned the chairman and said that my start was not very auspicious; was this something to worry about for the future? Edward Glover, always cool and calm, and wonderfully measured, said 'Don't worry – what do you suggest?' I said 'Let us have an afternoon service – Torah can be read and so forth.' He agreed and we phoned around and indeed the service was organised. I wrote a special prayer to commemorate Princess Diana, whom I considered to have been a very special person. I had started my journey with the community.

I did not move into the flat and I did not find an aged community – indeed I found many children and families, but we needed the help of everybody to bring together all members of the congregation. At the outset, we had twelve children enrolled in our religion school, boys and girls were bar/bat mitzvah at the age of fifteen or sixteen, and classes were held on Sunday mornings.

At my various interviews with the committee responsible for appointing a rabbi I emphasized that I would not do anything without a consensus; I wanted people to support what I was trying to achieve. And so I embarked on research about our community – the number of children, the ages of the members, etc. and gathered a lot of information. Evelyn and Albert were a great support and help, always ready and willing to assist. Indeed their support and encouragement were invaluable in my early years at Kent House. The research was not easy; it was time consuming, as we did not have our membership on a database, and all was done manually. But with the help of many, and not least my wife, we gathered the information and started to talk to members. Changes have occurred as the time has passed, and we now have over sixty children at Or Shabbat (as we call our religion school). Our children have their bar- and bat-mitzvah services at the age of thirteen (girls sometimes at twelve). With the help of our organist we have introduced new music and brought in a Selichot service, and our prayer book committee under the chairmanship of Professor Raphael has produced a new up-dated Pilgrim Festivals Prayer Book. I am hoping to have time and energy during my Sabbatical in 2004 to be well on the way to producing an up-dated version of our Rosh Hashanah Machzor.

HUGH SASSOON *was born in London to a 'Berkeley Street' family. In wartime he was shipped to Canada, returning in 1943 at the age of fourteen as a passenger on an aircraft carrier. Following National Service and university, he became a Chartered Accountant, banker and investment manager. He was also treasurer and chairman of a housing charity.*

In the mid-1940s (I was a teenager) I became aware of the very close relationship of my mother (who became Doris Herschorn) and the Reinharts – evidenced amongst other things by phone calls – both frequent and long – and over the years we saw a great deal of them. I was therefore well aware of the increasing tumult at the West London Synagogue which culminated in two special meetings at Friend's House with capacity, so it seemed, greater than that provided for High Holyday services including the inevitable overflows. This in itself tells something of the feelings generated.

Our revulsion in the way matters were handled (perhaps in reaction to Harold Reinhart being no angel when roused) and our desire to part from his enemies, led naturally to our joining in the foundation of his new congregation. That the break happened was brought home by the holding of High Holyday services in 1957 at Rudolph Steiner Hall, even before the formal founding of the new congregation.

My mother became immersed in the preparatory arrangements and was an initial member of the council. I was one of the first trustees – a position I held for some thirty-four years – and as such was asked to comment on sites being examined, particularly the Church of the Holy Shepherd in Lower Sloane Street, and later Kent House.

The first fund raising was an evening at the Kensington Palace Hotel when at the end of the proceedings I made a bid for the tombola left-overs. The pedal car which had attracted me was to be much enjoyed by a growing family, but what I had not appreciated was the volume of way out gramophone records and shirts and pyjamas of extreme sizes and equally extreme colours which came with it!

REMINISCENCES AND RECOLLECTIONS

Many members have enhanced this book with their memories of synagogue life. The few that follow come from a cross-section of the congregation.

CYNTHIA LANDES *and her husband Leonard first attended Westminster Synagogue in 1962 after seeing an announcement in* The Jewish Chronicle *for High Holyday services, but they were slow to make up their minds and did not become members until 1968. Leonard, who died in 1994, became junior warden in the year that Harold Reinhart died, and was still a warden when Albert Friedlander became the minister. Cynthia became a warden in 1984, the first woman to do so. Their daughter, Anna-Rose Jackson is also a member, although she now lives in Birmingham with her husband and two young sons.*

Mr Bradley, our first resident caretaker, had to go into hospital. Leonard, then senior warden, and I, in charge of hospitality, were summoned to Kent House, to be shown how to operate the huge safe in the kitchen. I still have a note of the manoeuvres needed to open and close the heavy door – so many half and quarter turns of the lever to the right or left. The door was always too heavy for me to manage, and I don't remember whether Leonard ever succeeded in following the instructions, but I still have them. Scrawled on an envelope and tucked into my hospitality notebook for 1970 and 1971, they are part of synagogue history. There, I noted that six dozen crusty rolls were ordered from Harrods, four (old) pence each, to be delivered on the morning of Tuesday, 9th June, for the Shavuot supper; that the small tea urn held thirty-five cups and the tall urn forty-two cups (according to the notes you could get twenty-four cups of coffee from a jar of Gold Blend Nescafe, cost six shillings).

lady agreed to come to Gibraltar and the Prince wrote to welcome her. Mme. Julie de St Laurent was to remain his beloved mistress for twenty-seven years, and whatever may be said about Prince Edward's behaviour, both then and later, there can be no doubt that they stayed closely attached to each other until, for reasons of state, they had to part.

Julie's background remains somewhat unclear. Edward referred to her at first as Mademoiselle, though she had certainly had earlier attachments. She was well bred, elegant and educated, and refused to be bought off when the Prince's entourage tried to disentangle him from the liaison. She accompanied him to Quebec when the king sent him there on a mission of state, and their establishment there was much like that of any other rather staid but affectionate married couple of their class. After visits to America, the West Indies and London the couple arrived in Halifax, Nova Scotia, where they found social convention less constricting than in Quebec. Edward's contact with his father was minimal. He was anxious that his position should be regularised, and was much concerned about Julie's future. He held no title and as usual was short of money. His establishment was now more extensive than it had been as a lone bachelor, but he could not return home to plead his cause without a summons from the king. He received no replies to his letters. 'I trust the time is not far distant,' he wrote, 'when I shall be permitted once more to approach you.' But no summons came. Finally the king did reply, but Edward's protest that the climate in Halifax was making him ill and that he needed his family's support, was ignored. In August 1798 the Prince had a nasty fall from his horse. He was at long last invited to return to England to take the waters at Bath and recuperate.

There was much concern about Edward's health. He was still limping from the fall but was nevertheless delighted to be back in London after an absence of thirteen years. His ever-present concerns about his income and his status were in the main responsible for his refusing to go to Bath. Julie was with him and the Royal family received him warmly, though of course without Madame, and he was honoured by civic dignitaries and old friends alike. His leg was improving and if only he could resolve his outstanding affairs he would be able to settle down and live quietly with his beloved mistress by his side.

A suite was prepared for the prince at Kensington Palace and he took rooms meanwhile at St James's; but where was Julie to live? She could certainly never take her place in court circles, nor could she stay with Edward in bachelor quarters. Across the park from the Palace, at the western end of Knightsbridge, stood a small but handsome house fronting on the main road, with gardens stretching as far as the back of the houses in Montpelier Street. The new Hyde Park Cavalry Barracks which had been erected only a few years earlier, were directly opposite There was much construction of barracks at this time, the nation being well aware of the discontents which had led to the French Revolution and previously to the loss of the American colonies. With one of the principal royal residences across the park it was important to have troops quartered close by; men billeted, as they often were, in private houses, were difficult to muster and too much exposed to radical influences. Edward found the Knightsbridge house suitable when refurbished as a home where he and Julie could relax happily in private, so he rented it from the leaseholder, a Mr Palmer. The prince still had no title, though his older brothers were already the Dukes of York and Clarence. He was expecting to be given the dukedom of Cumberland and was still peeved that his father had not granted him the financial privileges allowed to his brothers. Even his apartments at Kensington Palace were inadequately furnished. However, in April 1799 he was granted the dukedom of Kent, the Cumberland title going to his younger brother Ernest, and he was allowed £12,000 a year. He immediately named his property in Knightsbridge Kent House, after his own title.

The first Kent House occupied considerably more land than the present building. A builder and carpenter, George Shakespear, owned the whole plot fronting Kensington Road (the continuation of Knightsbridge), from the site of the present Rutland Court in the west, to Trevor Place, formerly Hill Street, in the east. On Hill Street stood a large floorcloth manufactory, next can predict the issues and the influences which will shape Anglo-Jewry in the coming decades. Nevertheless, the continued independence of Westminster Synagogue in a closely organised community will surely remain a valuable asset, and the synagogue's Statement of Principles and Policy will continue to guide its future.

help of members of the congregation; but happily the annual general meeting was able to welcome him back, with a warning that he must take life a little more easily! This injunction could not easily be obeyed, for the contractors were due to start work, and Renée Salamon was at the forefront of the refurbishment committee. However, by juggling her commitments, with several balls in the air at once, Renée managed to make the necessary arrangements for the work to begin.

It seemed at first that it might be necessary for the congregation to move out of the house while the builders were at work. Various temporary locations were considered, among them the German church in Kensington and an abandoned synagogue in Notting Hill; but it was felt by all concerned that however uncomfortable it might be, the congregation should 'camp out' at Kent House.

When the surveyors, architects and builders examined the house more closely, it became clear that the fabric was in a worse state than anyone had imagined. Parts of the exterior stonework were crumbling, the roof leaked, and the lift was considered unsafe. The refurbishment committee accordingly gave priority to essential aims – making the building weatherproof and safe, providing new classrooms and enabling the premises to be made sufficiently comfortable and efficient to attract additional income in the future. Tenders were invited for the work and a professional project manager appointed to oversee the operation.

Meanwhile the congregation was doing its best to maintain 'business as usual', and it was delighted to congratulate its rabbi emeritus on being awarded the OBE for his inter-faith work. Apart from Westminster Synagogue's own appreciation of his achievements, Rabbi Friedlander was warmly congratulated by leading members of non-Jewish organisations. Sister Margaret Shepherd, NDS, director of the Council of Christians and Jews, wrote a charming recollection of him: 'I remember marvelling at his ability to head a workshop at the annual Jewish-Christian-Muslim conference in Bendorf with his usual expertise and wisdom, whilst keeping a very young daughter, Nomi, happy as she played on his lap.' A few

Kent House lay empty for a while but was eventually taken as a town house by John Parker, 2nd Baron Borington, later Earl of Morley. He already had a splendid house, Saltram, in Devon, where he had entertained the king and queen. His sister, Theresa, had married George Villiers, the fourth son of the lst Earl of Clarendon. Known in family circles as Mrs George, she and her family came to live at Kent House with the Morleys. To accommodate the large family of Parkers and Villiers, and preserve each family's privacy while sharing some of the expenses, the house was split down the middle. Described as 'large, spacious and dignified', Kent House comfortably housed them all, and the large gardens were much enjoyed, particularly by the children. One communicating door apparently remained open and the Villiers children were especially fond of their aunt Morley, who was so easily reached.

For some sixty years Kent House was one of Victorian London's most prominent centres of political, artistic and social life. Both the Morleys and the Villiers were involved in parliamentary affairs. Lord Canning was a frequent visitor, and the lengthy debates on the Corn Laws, in which Clarendon was deeply involved, must have been thrashed out there after he succeeded to the title in 1838. Mrs George, too, was an incisive and witty commentator on the social scene. Her daughter, alsoTheresa, took after her mother as a bright, intelligent and well-read young lady, used to moving in the highest political and literary circles. In her parents' eyes of course no young man was quite good enough for their daughter, but in 1830 she married Thomas Lister. He died twelve years later leaving her with three children, but within two years she married George Cornewall Lewis, and they too made Kent House (the western half) their home. Lewis had a distinguished career in the Commons, becoming Chancellor of the Exchequer in Lord Palmerston's first administration, in succession to Mr Gladstone, though one political commentator described him as 'cold-blooded as a fish'. Nevertheless, Theresa seemed perfectly contented, making herself busy at Kent House writing and visiting and creating something of a 'salon' amongst their many distinguished friends. She published in three volumes *The Lives of the Friends and Contemporaries of Lord Chancellor Clarendon,* her ancestor, and she edited the papers of Lady Mary Berry, which her father-in-law, Sir Thomas Lewis, had inherited.

Knightsbridge and Kensington had become highly fashionable by the middle of the century. A young and popular royal family now occupied Kensington Palace, and across the road from Kent House, on the far side of the barracks and visible from all the upper windows, stood the magnificent Crystal Palace where the Great Exhibition opened in 1851; the world flocked to see the evidence of Britain's industrial splendour. Sir George Cornewall Lewis died in 1863 and his wife two years later, and few were then left who could remember Kent House in its great days. The freehold had been acquired by Mitchell Henry, the occupier of Stratheden House, on the opposite side of Rutland Gardens, and in 1870, with a view to an ambitious development of the whole area, the 'substantial mansion' was demolished.

The plot of land where Kent House had stood was bought by Louisa, Lady Ashburton. Like most of the chatelaines of Kent House, Louisa was intelligent and well-read. She had always moved in wealthy and artistic circles but she had a streak of eccentricity and was not universally well liked. Her great grandfather was a Sephardi Jew, Ephraim Baron D'Aguilar, a wealthy Portuguese who married Sarah da Costa and lived in London with his wife and their two daughters, Caroline and Georgina, Louisa's grandmother. When his wife died D'Aguilar married again, but gradually his mental health deteriorated and he became so miserly and so cruel to his family that they could no longer tolerate him. He bought a small farm in Islington and treated his animals so appallingly that the place was known as Starvation Farm. He died, still wealthy, in disgusting conditions, refusing to see his daughter Caroline when she called. He had made no will so his fortune was inherited by Caroline and her sister.

Georgina married Admiral Keith Stewart, a Scottish landowner, and their son James married Mary Mackenzie, a widow, joining his name to hers. Their

THE RABBI RECOLLECTS . . .

It was a warm summer's day in 1996 when Rabbi Albert Friedlander and I had lunch in a small restaurant on Old Brompton Road. During that very pleasant lunch I mentioned to him that I would like to return to more full-time rabbinic work and at the same time I asked him if he had any suggestions. He looked at me and said that he was retiring and that there was going to be vacancy at Westminster Synagogue. I must admit that at that time I knew very little about Westminster, so I said that I would think about this. I started my research, and my first ports of call were several of my colleagues from both of the rabbinic movements: the Rabbinic Conference and the Assembly of Rabbis, Liberal and Reform groups respectively. I asked them what they knew about the community and without exception they told me that if I were to take the position I would get a beautiful flat in Knightsbridge and virtually rest on my laurels, as there would be very little to do: a dwindling independent community, elderly people, and so forth.

It was in September 1997, over a year from the moment of my lunch with Albert, when I took up my position at the synagogue. Indeed, it was on 16 April, 1997, my son's birthday, that the congregation decided to appoint me to succeed Rabbi Friedlander and become the community's third minister in its forty years history.

My first service was scheduled to be on Saturday, 6 September 1997, the day of the funeral of Diana, Princess of Wales, who died tragically in a car accident in Paris on 31 August of that year. So here was my first crisis: Knightsbridge was on the route of the funeral cortege and all surrounding streets were closed, so how were we going to hold our morning service? I phoned the chairman and said that my start was not very auspicious; was in the synagogue people who know me, who will always greet me, and a place that will be both theirs and mine for some time to come. As I become more and more a member of the community, I feel a sense of satisfaction that through my (attempts at) teaching, I am welcoming others into the same environment that I have learned to feel at home in. Teaching has strengthened me (physically as well as mentally), and through it I hope and believe that both my pupils and I have benefited.

EDWARD GLOVER *is married to Juliet; they have two children, Leo and Samantha, three dogs and six cats. He is a career property financier and investor and is a director and head of property for HSBC Specialist Investments Ltd. He is interested in cricket, which he refuses to give up, and has been involved in the Maccabi movement including stints as chairman of Maccabi Association and vice-chairman of Maccabi Great Britain.*

My mother was brought up in a largely non-observant household. In deference to my father, president of the Bournemouth Hebrew Congregation (though he always said that this was because the members thought they were voting for his father!) she had been married under orthodox auspices; but she had never been really comfortable in an orthodox environment or with the idea of bringing up her son in it. As a precocious eight-year-old, I had also been distinctly unimpressed by my first experiences of an orthodox congregation, so the invitation from a neighbour to try out a new Reform synagogue within walking distance, presided over by Rabbi Reinhart, of whom my mother had passing knowledge, was timely and eagerly taken up. Westminster Synagogue had only recently been established in its intended permanent home, but both community and building made immediate and lasting impressions.

The services were a revelation. They were short and understandable, with both Hebrew and English read clearly and with expression. They were conducted with a precision of which Sir Malcolm Sargeant would have been proud, but the decorum and attention which this encouraged from the

14. *The original barrel-vaulted ceiling and marble floor of the entrance hall*

Sir Coutts all involved, to say nothing of Louisa herself, it was surprising that the house was ever completed. Carlyle, still a close friend, described Clutton as 'that arch-quack and son of Beelzebub'. The new Kent House, with its grounds, was much smaller than its predecessor, covering much the same area as it does today, except for the stables through the archway at the end of the newly built Rutland Gardens. With her usual extravagance Louisa wanted space for eight horses and six carriages, and rooms for coachmen and grooms. She was persuaded to tone down her demands a little, but still managed to ensure that the establishment was suitable for herself and her daughter.

Any well-designed town house of the period was expected to provide rooms on the ground floor or in the basement for the gentlemen of the household: billiards room, smoking room and study. Clutton, allowing for this, had arranged for all the public rooms to be on the first floor, but now that Browning and other possible suitors had withdrawn, and Louisa and Maysie were on their own, he changed the arrangements. The main entrance porch was where it is today; carriages could pull up safely for their passengers to alight, and then continue down the road to the new stable block. Through the little entrance lobby, the hall led straight ahead into what is known today as the Knightsbridge room. The marble hall, constructed as a perfect cube, led into the dining-room. The proportions of this room were splendid, with plaster cornices running right round the ceiling, and at the far end a dumb-waiter (still present) gave access to the offices in the basement and to the reception rooms above. Against the left wall stood the great ebony and ormolu chimney-piece, now serving as the Holy Ark in the sanctuary. Above the black mantle appeared the words: Eat to live and live to serve. Louisa's usual habit of changing her mind led to the dining-room ceiling being raised after completion, at an additional cost of £1,300. There has been much debate about the wallpaper in the dining-room. It was generally believed to be of gold repoussée leather, seen later in what was known as Whistler's Peacock Room. The Noble family, who bought the house after Louisa's death, certainly thought so, but during recent refurbishment it congregant, my then fiancé Christopher, with him. Then there were the years of small Reeses getting under everyone's feet and on some people's nerves, as we tested to extremes that the Westminster welcome was extended to all ages. Ours was, I believe the first wedding that Albert celebrated at Kent House. Our daughter Clare's to Yuval Keren – was by a happy coincidence the last before he retired.

And now again a new era in synagogue life, only this time I suppose we must count among the 'elders'. But that original flavour of spiritual strength and great vibrancy that made itself felt in 1961, has survived all the outward changes that the years have brought to Kent House; I am as proud to share the prospect of the next four decades as I am to look back on those past.

ALEXANDER GOLDSMITH, *16, is in the midst of his AS levels at St Benedict's school, Ealing. He enjoys reading, playing the piano, and is a member of the Air Cadets; he assists with teaching the six to seven year old group at Kent House on Saturday mornings.*

From a very early age, I can remember sitting with my father in our familiar seats (which have at times been usurped, always to be zealously reclaimed). At first, going to the synagogue meant that I would sit, slightly fidgety, waiting for the sermon, and the subsequent Kiddush, and of course, challah. However, some things intrigued me; I would sit forward in my chair for my favourite songs, and crane my neck to see the scrolls pass, and their elevation. My father would discuss the portion with me in the afternoon (if my concentration held for long enough!) and so a pleasant routine was built into Saturdays.

Gradually, I learnt more about Judaism, and about why we were at the synagogue. I started to engage with the community, with the services, and with the ideas that I came across. The synagogue is still something that is reassuringly constant in my life, as the exams flash by or loom ahead, as work mounts up or is, at a slower rate, completed. I know that I shall find

It was about this time that Ralph Yablon devised a plan to warehouse shares in a hitherto family company which was being reshaped to go public. In parallel with others, I guaranteed a bank loan, the resulting overall profit of the scheme going a long way to cover the cost of Kent House. At about 9 pm, on two occasions, I found Harold Reinhart at my door, and knowing he never took no for an answer I was fearful he would sit out the night if necessary. The first request was for funds to pay for the Everlasting Light he had just bought; the second was for half of the cost of the first organ. No doubt he did this to others also.

The new synagogue was made by, and has prospered through, the tireless efforts of Harold Reinhart and many others, then and since. However, there was certainly one fundamental problem, not tackled in time: the attitude to teaching in the early days of the religion school; it is good to know that this aspect of synagogue life has now greatly changed.

EZRA DINGOOR *was born in Bombay of Iraqi parents. He came to England in 1953 and became a mechanical engineer. After National Service he joined the British Coal Utilisation Research Association and later the Central Electricity Generating Board, representing the UK on the International Electricity Council. He became a J.P. in 1984 and is a Trustee of Age Concern, Barnet. He married Eileen at Kent House in 1961 and they have two children.*

My earliest memory was of attending services at Caxton Hall; I distinctly remember the little Ark being brought into the small room for prayers. Then we moved to the exciting phase of acquiring Kent House. I had never seen so much dust and dirt, and it was marvellous to witness the dignity of labour. No task was too cumbersome. Everyone was willing to apply rust remover on to fireplaces and to clean the marble. It was patently obvious that Mrs Reinhart had done nothing like it in her life, but that did not prevent her from tackling the job with gusto! My wife Eileen and I were the first to be married in Kent House in October, 1960.

When I was appointed as warden for the first time, I recall that Peter

15. *The old Victorian safe in the kitchen*

the 'war effort' in 1939. The first floor rooms had balustraded stone balconies, and the second floor handsome iron ones.

On the ground floor Blomfield broke through the right hand wall of the lobby to extend the entrance hall, and the family used the present Knightsbridge room as a morning room. The architect also raised the ceiling with the lantern skylight above the staircase. The dining room remained almost as Lady Ashburton had left it, but her Turners and Titians had gone. The Saxtons' love of music led to the construction on the first floor of an impressive room for this purpose. To make this possible the wall between two of the reception rooms overlooking Rutland Gardens was knocked down, but Blomfield's plan for a pillared screen with an archway 'so that the sound would pass well from one part to another' was frustrated by the discovery of a steel girder running across the room where the dividing wall had stood. The entablature was therefore taken right around the double room, almost seventy feet long, decorated with festoons in plasterwork, the whole lit by splendid French crystal chandeliers.

Beautiful though the music room was, Celia and Saxton thought that something was lacking. Their own possessions could hardly fill such a large space, and though they bought more furniture, pictures and ornaments, they could not match the imposing scale of Louisa Ashburton's purchases. Saxton had been introduced in Paris to the Catalan artist José-Maria Sert, and commissioned him to fill the walls of the first floor of Kent House with a series of paintings in whatever style he thought best. The work was carried out in the Paris studio without the Saxtons even seeing the paintings. Sert himself brought them to London and saw them safely set in place. This was the artist's first London commission, to be followed later by work on Sir Philip Sassoon's house in Park Lane, and by further paintings for the Nobles at their country home Wretham Hall in Norfolk. Although the Kent House panels are fully described and illustrated in Alberto del Castillo's book, *José-Maria Sert, Su Vida y su Obra*, the most vivid account in English is that of Sir Humphrey Noble himself: 'In the first room, the decoration completely covers the whole wall, ignoring doors, windows and fireplace, the colour being gold and brown. At one end of the room there seems to be a canal stretching away into the distance, with bridges and elephants lining the banks (he was very fond of elephants and camels and strange birds); a large barge is approaching and all sorts of fireworks, rockets and Catherine wheels are being let off. On another wall, people are bringing presents to some royal couple and behind them are seen precipitous and impossible mountains on which are perched classical temples, while over the columns are painted the architrave and cornice on which little 'putti' are letting off fire-arms, in a very dangerous manner, it must be admitted. In the next room the colour of the walls was of lapis lazuli and the pictures, always in gold and brown, were fixed to the walls.' Sert wanted the rooms to be finished in time for a performance of Richard Strauss's music for Diaghilev's *Légende de Joseph* for which he had provided the décor, and Strauss himself came to Kent House, using 'an elegant lorgnette' to see the murals.

The whole house was elaborately furnished with vast Chinese screens, Japanese gongs and other embellishments brought back from many visits abroad. Later Celia and Saxton lived somewhat separate lives (he had a mistress in Monte Carlo) but at Kent House they gave grand parties and musical soirées, and entertained many distinguished musical and theatrical guests. Mrs Madan (Celia's sister) recalled visits by Pablo Casals and his first wife Suggia; Donald Tovey, the violinist and musicologist; Diaghilev and several of his company; Myra Hess, Irene Scharrer, Mrs Patrick Campbell, Lady Tree and the American music-hall singer, Ethel Levy. Dinner parties in the splendid dining-room were huge, with twenty guests or more at a time. After brief introductions upstairs (the Saxtons disapproved of cocktails), the gentlemen, in full evening dress, escorted the ladies down to dinner. 'On the table with a gleaming white cloth,' Sir Humphrey recalled, 'were arranged silver pieces, cups, centre-pieces, bon-bon dishes, great spoons which could never be used, candlesticks and dishes of fruit which would be handed round at the end of the meal, salt-cellars, pepper pots and flowers.' At least twelve live-in servants were needed: butler, cooks, maidservants, bootboy and extra help when guests were expected. One visitor to a ball at Kent House in the 1920s was Frank Waley, the first Chairman of Westminster Synagogue.

Leon Goossens, writing in *The Times* on the death of Sir Humphrey Noble, recalls meeting the family at Covent Garden where they had regular seats in the front of the stalls. He was invited back to Kent House to meet Lotte Lehmann, Elizabeth Schumann and Fredrick Schorr. Another visitor was Princess Marie-Louise, Queen Victoria's grand-daughter. She had a miserable marriage, divorcing her German husband on grounds of cruelty, something of a scandal at the time. She lived in rather reduced circumstances at a ladies' club, but on hearing of her unhappiness Celia, an old friend, invited her to stay at Kent House. She remained there for two years 'insisting on being godmother to all the grandchildren, and holding the baby at the christening.' She died in 1956, much missed by the Saxtons.

In 1940 Celia and Saxton left Kent House to live in Bath. Their last dinner party, recorded by Sir Humphrey, was held just before war broke out. Those present included Lady Melchett (Louisa Ashburton's house, Melchet in Hampshire, had been bought by Sir Alfred Mond, founder of ICI, who had

16. *Floor plans of Kent House as it was in 1907 and 1913*

17. *The original wrought-iron balustrade on the first floor*

adopted its name as Lord Melchett), the Marchioness of Reading, Colonel and Mrs Bowes-Lyon, Harold Nicolson, Countess Jellicoe and the Japanese Ambassador and Mme Yoshida. To save the house from being requisitioned the Nobles had offered it to the Red Cross as a storage depot. Saxton died in 1942, but Celia survived until 1962. Her funeral was in Bath Abbey. In Bath she had enjoyed a deliberately uncomfortable old age. Her daughter, Lady Gladwyn, remembered: 'She likes to sit in a howling draught, hardly to eat, never to heat a room or soak herself in a hot bath, to have yapping dachshunds all over the sofas and chairs.' Perhaps the situation had been the same at Kent House.

Towards the end of the war the house was taken over by Telephone Rentals Ltd. Mrs Madan recalled the typists 'tapping away below the Sert gods and goddesses'. Saxton Noble had asked the artist to make the panels removable in case of flood or fire, but only the north wall was so constructed. The south wall panels were firmly fixed. The Nobles' family chauffeur was still living in the basement 'making tea for the typists'. The Sert murals are believed to be now in Spain. The house may never again contain such splendours as it did in previous times, but at least it is cared for and its walls resound once more with music and debate. Its previous owners would surely approve of the use to which it has been put.

FURTHER READING

Chancellor, E. C., *Knightsbridge and Belgravia*, 1909

Gillen, Mollie, *The Prince and His Lady*, 1970

Jebb, Miles (ed.), *The Diaries of Cynthia Gladwyn*, 1995

Noble, Humphrey, *Life in Noble Houses*, 1967

Surtees, Virginia, *The Ludovisi Goddess – The Life of Louisa, Lady Ashburton*, 1984

The Survey of London, Vol. 45, *Knightsbridge*, 2000

APPENDICES

APPENDIX A

THE CHAGALL LITHOGRAPHS

The Twelve Tribes of Israel

Marc Chagall's twelve stained glass windows, commissioned by the Women's Zionist Organisation of America for the synagogue of the Hadassah Hebrew University Medical Centre in Jerusalem, were executed in Rheims in 1961. In the same year, Chagall created lithographs of the window designs, limited to one hundred and fifty copies, each numbered and signed by the artist. Mr R. C. Yablon generously presented a set of these lithographs to Westminster Synagogue, where they now adorn the synagogue library. The stained glass windows are of heroic size, each eleven feet high and eight feet across. The lithographs are twenty-four inches high and eighteen inches across. With due allowance for the great reduction in size and the total difference of the medium, the lithographs convey the message of the windows, being identical in detail and conveying what has been called the singing quality of the colours.

The pictures represent the twelve tribes of ancient Israel, sprung from the twelve sons of Jacob. The imagery suggests Jacob's blessings on the sons as recorded in the forty-ninth chapter of Genesis, with some references to Moses' blessing of the tribes as told in the thirty-third chapter of Deuteronomy; but the forms derive mainly from Chagall's own genius, nourished by the intense Jewish life of Vitebsk in his native Russia, and by characteristic trends in contemporary art.

I

In Westminster Synagogue, the series starts with the picture nearest the window on the east wall: Reuben. Eight of the twelve pictures contain quotations in the original Hebrew from the blessing of Jacob. On the Reuben picture, Chagall inscribes 'Reuben, thou art my first-born, my might and the first-fruits of my strength, the excellency of dignity..' The light blue colour is itself suggestive of the character: openhearted, impetuous, unstable. The solar disc betokens latent strength; and birds and fish are evidence of welfare, with small images of sheep indicating the pastoral destiny of the tribe.

II

Following around to the right, Simeon is next. The blue of this picture is dark and stormy. Across the bottom is spread the ominous verse: 'Simeon and Levi are brothers; weapons of violence are their swords. Let not my soul come into their secret.' But, for Chagall, the verse and the character are reserved for Simeon alone. The winged horse, the winged bull are charging: and birds fly from the frightening scene. The round globe quivers, and trees and houses in the darkening background quake. From a corner peers a single knowing eye.

III

For Levi, Chagall selects a shining sunlit background, and for Levi alone, a text not from Jacob's blessing, but from Moses: 'They shall teach Jacob thine ordinances, and Israel thy laws; they shall set incense before thee, and whole burnt offerings upon thine altar. Bless, Lord, his substance, and the work of—' The verse is inscribed on two tables of stone in the form always pictured for the Ten Words; and round about are serried rows of candles in sacred flame, while above, all nature – bird and beast and leaf and flower – rejoices. Above the flowers and flanked by birds, appears, perhaps gratuitously, a six-pointed star.

IV

In the fourth picture, the formidable lion of Judah crouches in a blood-red field, his head surmounted as with a crown, by a view of the holy city, while high above, great spreading hands lift up a conventional crown of crimson hue, even darker than the surrounding field and inscribed: Judah. The whole suggests splendour and power; and before the lion's head appear the words: 'Thy brethren shall praise thee; thy hand shall be on the neck . . .'

V

The name Zebulun appears in great gold letters in the red sky above the red sea, the scene of maritime prosperity. The red sun and the red moon shine from the red horizon upon ships and fishes, gay and flourishing. No verse is quoted here.

VI

Issachar is portrayed in calm soft green; a fertile plain with pleasant habitation, fowl and flocks, and an all-encircling vine. The verse: 'Issachar is a strong ass crouching between the sheepfolds' is inscribed on a white apex supported by hands of blessing. At the base of the picture is seen the ass, dozing in his comfort and lightly bearing the burden of his tribute in the form of a gentle dove.

VII

Many colours play among the prevailing blues of the Dan picture. The legend 'Dan shall judge his people, as one of the tribes of Israel' appears across the arched top and down the left side to the base, whence springs a candelabrum of enlightenment. The serpent, suggestive of 'the adder in the path' coiling about the candlestick probably hints also at the wisdom behind justice; and the sword and the balances held aloft symbolise also judgement. Beasts and birds and buildings and fish and foliage afford glimpses of the variety and mystery of the world in which justice must be sought.

VIII

'Gad, a troop shall band against him; but he shall wound their heel' is the verse which illumines top and centre of the next picture, the prevailing colour of which is the green of this pastoral tribe. Great splashes of sombre red symbolise the violence of the aggressors round about, depicted here as fantastic beasts of many sorts, before whom, behind an impregnable shield, a crowned eagle, wings outstretched, foreshadows the final victory.

IX

The crowned eagle is the central image also in the next picture, that of Asher, full brother of Gad. But in all other respects the representation differs. Here is a bright and affluent scene, in which peace reigns. Bright flowers are abundant. Olive trees appear with the seven-branched lamp between them (as in the vision of Zechariah), and overall, a dove of multi-coloured plumage flies with an olive branch upon the scene of lush and loving life. 'Asher', we read, 'his bread shall be fat, and he shall yield royal dainties.'

X

No text, except for the single word Naphtali, appears on the next picture. In the blessing of Jacob, 'Naphtali is a hind let loose; he gives goodly words.' The picture shows the hind, in a handsome red coat recumbent, with a watchful eye on the gay scene, in which a luxuriant tree rises to a gorgeous fighting cock, all on a background of sunny light.

XI

For Joseph alone is reserved a pattern of richest orange and golden hues embracing a multitude of symbols of prosperity and blessing. The fruitful bough springs above the well; and huge grapes abundant overflow the wall. Flocks graze contentedly within sight of the radiant city. Joseph's 'firm bow' is poised centrally in the hand of a crowned dove; and at the very summit, hands of blessing hold the horn of salvation.

XII

In the final picture, Benjamin, appear fragments of the verse 'Benjamin is a ravening wolf, in the morning devouring the prey, in the evening dividing the spoil.' The ravening beast stands sated over his prey; and the usual birds, fish and animals appear. Just above the haunch of the beast we glimpse a view of the glorious city. The entire centre of the Benjamin picture is occupied by a huge ring in which smaller curves surround a central circle, suggesting the inclusion in the whole of Israel of the so-different tribes which compose it, and perhaps also hinting at the 'wheels' of Ezekiel's mystic vision.

H.F.R.

The Presidents of the Synagogue

1957–1968	Seymour Karminski
1969–1974	Frank Waley
1974–1980	Ralph Yablon
1980–1990	Lewis Golden
1990–2000	Ivor Connick
2000–	Cynthia Landes

The Chairmen of the Council

1957–1968	Frank Waley
1968–1971	Lewis Golden
1971	Albert Polack
1971–1974	Leo Bernard
1975–1976	Ivor Connick
1977–1979	Hugh Sassoon
1979–1981	Constance Stuart
1981–1985	John Rochman
1985–1987	Aryan Kahane
1987–1989	David Raphael
1989–1991	Christopher Rees
1991–1995	Ezra Dingoor
1996–2000	Edward Glover
2000–	Howard Leigh

INDEX